TRAILS
To
Timberline
In
West Central
British Columbia

By Einar Blix

ISBN 0-88925-969-0

Guide maps by Einar Blix
Photographs, unless otherwise credited, by Einar Blix
Printed by D.W. Friesen, Cloverdale, B.C.

Publisher: Fjelltur Books, Box 2604, Smithers, British Columbia, Canada V0J 2N0

Printed and bound in Canada

Canadian Cataloguing in Publication Data

Blix, Einar, 1930-
   Trails to timberline in west central
British Columbia

   ISBN 0-88925-969-0

   1. Trails - British Columbia - Guide-books.
2. Hiking - British Columbia - Guide-books.
3. British Columbia - Descriptive and travel -
1981-   - Guide-books.* I. Title.
GV199.44.C22B753 1989   917.11'32   C89-091432-X

By same author, More Trails to Timberline, 1994
ISBN 1-55056-288-6

To Andrew, Nancy & Lorna

that they and their generation

may know and enjoy the wilderness

and cherish it for those yet to come.

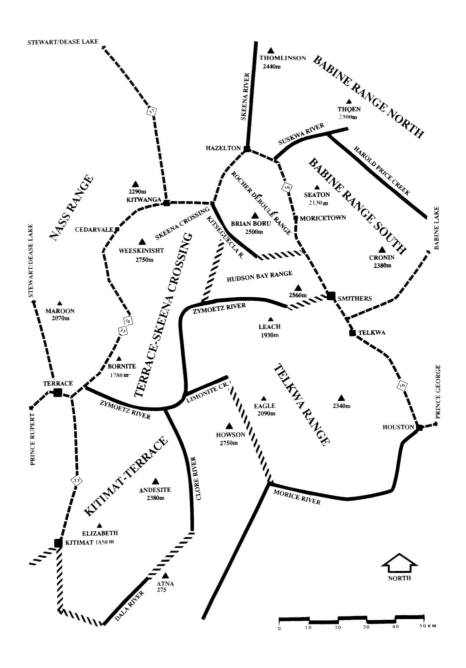

West Central British Columbia
GENERAL AREA AND SUBDIVISIONS

CONTENTS
[See also "More Trails to Timberline" (27)]

FOREWORD

The main purpose of this book is to stimulate interest and participation in outdoor activities, such as hiking and ski touring, by making information more readily available on access routes to alpine areas.

For those who may find it more rewarding to know something about the origin and history of the trails and roads they are treading, I have included a few notes on historical and natural features. Some helpful hints on clothing and equipment have been included for the benefit of novices and for newcomers to the area, who may not be familiar with the vagaries of the climate. Such notes are not intended to probe deeply into any topic, but simply to provide some answers to fairly obvious questions.

Most of the material is factual and objective, but inevitably, the presentation and contents are coloured by my own experince and convictions. I make no apology for that. It is by virtue of more than 30 years as a resident, variously of Kemano, Kitimat, Terrace and Smithers, and many more years of experience in hiking, skiing and a wide range of other outdoor activities, plus the experience of bringing up a family to know and enjoy the outdoors, that I feel qualified to write this book.

Over the years, I have been fortunate enough to travel quite extensively and live in various parts of the world. Such experience has convinced me that we are indeed privileged to live in a unique area. The magnificent and still largely unspoilt wilderness at our doorstep offers some of the best hiking, skiing, mountaineering and other outdoor recreation to be found anywhere. Obviously, and fortunately, not everyone would agree that those opportunities compensate for the disadvantages of living in this relatively isolated area, but it is becoming clear that more and more do.

I have attempted to identify features that make some trails particularly suitable for families with children. So many of our recreational activities tend to disrupt family life, but hiking and skiing can be shared and enjoyed by young and old, and at a cost that most families can afford. Apart from uniting families and generations, active forms of outdoor recreation are a direct investment in preventive medicine, mental and physical, with an exceptionally good rate of return. It is an investment that society cannot afford to ignore, but must promote vigourously.

It would be surprising if there were no errors or omissions. Certainly, in many instances the reader will disagree with my assessment of trail condition, degree of difficulty, time requirement and so on. I can only ask such critics for their indulgence and understanding.

Some people may disagree entirely with the concept of publishing comprehensive information about trails and other access routes to alpine areas. With such critics I take issue. Most of them feel strongly about preserving the environment and will argue that to publicize access routes is to invite trouble. They fear the mountains will be over-run by people who do not know or care about how to behave to avoid harming the environment, or who will hurt themselves or get lost. Above all, they wish to avoid the risk that snowmobiles, trailbikes and the like will find their way up into the mountains and do damage to plants and animals.

I have great sympathy for that line of argument and am also concerned about the risk to the environment. However, the more powerful counter-argument is that unless far more people are persuaded to actively enjoy the recreation potential of our mountains and become committed to the preservation of that environment, its degradation is inevitable rather than a controlable risk. Without large numbers of concerned and well informed residents, organized into effective groups, our alpine areas and access to them, in reality, have no protection. A few isolated individual, no matter how dedicated, cannot stop or control commercial exploitation of resources in those sensitive, but little used areas. Nor should they expect to have exclusive use of large areas that may have many potential uses and users.

If the best use of our alpine areas is for recreation, the only way to ensure that they are primarily reserved for that purpose, is for enough people to say so. How can enough people be brought around to that point of view if they remain ignorant about access routes and have no encouragement to enjoy the recreational opportunities that are available? Those who already possess the necessary knowledge and experience have a responsibility to share it with others who do not. The full measure of that responsibility cannot be discharged by experts acting in isolation. It takes well organized groups of committed, knowledgeable people to provide the leadership and training required to, among other things, promote hiking and ski touring, keep access information up-to-date, ensure that trails are kept in good repair, influence resource management, negotiate agreements or compromises with other resource users and make sure enough qualified individuals can be made available at short notice to assist with search and rescue operations.

Management decisions cannot, of course, always favour outdoor recreation over all other resource uses, nor can the environment everywhere be preserved in its natural state at any cost. The goal must be to exploit our resources sensibly and to the extent necessary to support a population that is sufficient to control the process, but not so large that the quality of life and the environment are seriously degraded. Maintaining an adequate population, without allowing numbers to rise to the point where the territory becomes a worthless wasteland, is a timeless and universal problem. It is faced by every living organism, but only humanity has not been content to leave control of the process to "nature". Time alone will tell if we can do better. Indications so far are not encouraging, but there is no way back, so we must keep trying.

ACKNOWLEDGEMENTS

It would be impossible to adequately acknowledge all the help and encouragement I have received from various people, but I must make specific reference to some. First of all, this book could not have been written without the help and enthusiastic support I received from my wife and family. The Aluminum Company of Canada Ltd. was most helpful and understanding and contributed greatly to the success of the project. A grant from Canada Council came at a time when material and moral support were much needed and I gratefully acknowledge that expression of faith in this book. I also want to thank Mary Baker (then) of Kitimat, Ray Parfitt (then) of Terrace and Bill Bryant of Smithers for their help and encouragement.

SECOND EDITION ADDENDUM

Because of the many positive comments directed to me about the book and the fact that the first edition is both out of print and out of date, I decided to go ahead with a revised edition.

So many things have changed in the dozen years since the book was first published. Access to alpine areas has changed, in some cases for the better and in other cases for the worse. Nature and man have both been agents of change. The interest in active forms of outdoor recreation has grown at a phenomenal rate. It is just wonderful to see so many people enjoying hiking and ski touring. To hear so many area residents now talking about winter as a season of great opportunities for outdoor activities, instead of a time to be dreaded, is a particularly welcome change.

With the widespread use of mountain bikes, a whole new field of outdoor recreation has opened up and in addition, it has made access to many alpine areas much easier. Steady improvement has taken place in all outdoor recreation equipment. It is stronger, lighter and the variety is staggering.

Above all attitudes, to the environment, resource management, physical fitness and the value of tourism, to mention just a few examples, have changed and are continuing to change very significantly. Not enough yet to ensure our survival, but in the right direction.

Apart from updating the information on alpine access routes, I have added some new ones and omitted others that I no longer consider worthwhile. References to a number of recent publications pertaining to this area have been included. Since all maps are gradually being converted from Imperial to metric measures, I have switched to metric in this edition. However, many older maps are still in use, so I have included conversion tables at the back of the book. Not surprisingly, I have also found it necessary or desireable to make a number of editorial changes that will hopefully be seen as improvements by the readers as well.

Smithers, B.C.
May, 1989.

GEOGRAPHY AND CLIMATE

The area referred to in this book as West Central British Columbia, has no well defined or generally accepted geographical boundaries. It is often spoken of as Northwest B.C., but in terms of its real geographical location, that designation is clearly erroneous. The fact is that Highway 16, which is the point of departure for most of these trails to timberline, cuts across the Province slightly south of the half-way mark between the U.S. and Yukon borders. For present purposes, West Central British Columbia has been defined as the area bounded in the north by the Babine River and a line drawn westwards from its junction with the Skeena; a line running south to Kitimat, from the intersection of the northern boundary and the Nass River, marks the western boundary; the Dala and Morice Rivers form the southern boundary and on the east side, the outline is completed by a line joining the Morice River at Houston and Babine Lake. Very roughly, the overall dimensions of the area are 120 by 180 km.

It has not been possible to cover the whole of that large area with equal emphasis. I have concentrated mainly on a corridor, not much more than 100 km wide, along Highway 16, from Telkwa in the east to Terrace in the west. It includes most of the best hiking, mountaineering and ski touring country in the region and is within reasonable travelling distance for the great majority of residents.

The stylized General Area map facing the Contents page shows the subdivision into smaller areas for the purpose of organizing this book. Access considerations have largely determined the subdivision boundaries.

The topography is everywhere dominated by mountains separated by deep, narrow valleys. Compared with the lofty peaks found in the Rockies, in Alaska and farther south in the Coast Range, the local mountains are quite modest. A few rise to almost 2800 m, but most are in the 1800 to 2200 m range. However, since the base elevation is not much above sea level, they are no less impressive than the Rockies, where the base is about 1000 m. Going east, the base elevation does rise gradually to meet the Interior Plateau, but in any case, the more easterly mountains tend to occur as isolated, relatively low, rounded formations.

When seen from a high vantage point or from the air, the most striking feature is the enormous expanse of snowfields and glaciers in all directions. Even at the height of summer, the valleys appear as narrow, dark ribbons in an otherwise white world.

The mountains are young. The streams are still fast-flowing and violent, transporting a heavy load of abrasive material that is carving the canyons steadily deeper. Rocks, mud, snow and ice rumbling down the steep slopes do their part in wearing down the land. How the mountains were formed in the first place and the geology of this area in general, is a fascinating story. For anyone who wants to delve into it, there is no better starting point than Allen

5

Gottesfeld's recent book "Geology of the Northwest Mainland" (1).

All the forces of nature at work cannot be safely ignored by those who aspire to see and experience the mountains at close quarters. Avalanches probably pose the greatest hazard for the unwary. On the time scale of natural phenomena, they occur quite frequently. The dynamics are complex and not completely understood, even by the experts. Others should definitely regard avalanches as highly unpredictable events. Where there is snow or ice above on a steep slope, make a detour if possible. The hazard is usually greatest in late winter and spring, when the accumulation of snow at higher elevations is at a maximum and the snow is most unstable. However, there is no guarantee that similar or worse conditions may not be encountered at other times of the year!

The climate in this area is such that the potential for all kinds of weather records and freak conditions is virtually unlimited. It is next to impossible to define "normal" patterns. To some extent, the whole area is affected by moisture-laden, Pacific air. Combined with other influences, this produces a gradual transition, from the mild, wet conditions that usually prevail west of the Coast Range mountains to the drier, harsher climate of the interior. The Coast Range mountains themselves have a pronounced influence. When mild, moist Pacific air comes up against them, it is forced upwards where it cools and moisture condenses. The result is the heavy rain and snowfalls so characteristic of the western slopes. By the time it gets across the mountains, the air is cooler and drier. Another important factor is the huge land mass of the North American continent to the east. It tends to generate large volumes of dry air, cold in the winter and hot in the summer, that flows out from the resulting high pressure centres towards low pressure areas over the Pacific Ocean. West Central British Columbia is often the battlefield where air masses from the interior and the Pacific clash. As the battle surges to and fro, the weather is dominated in turn by one, then the other. The net result is that conditions are very difficult to predict, change rapidly and can vary widely between areas separated by only a few kilometers. Even west of the Coast Mountains, where extremes of temperature are rare, the odd summer produces months of uninterrupted, hot, dry weather and the occasional winter brings prolonged periods of clear, cold conditions.

The vegetation below timberline and particularly in the valley bottoms, varies from fairly dense to impenetrable. Moving inland from the coast, the going tends to get a little easier, but at the same time timberline moves up from about 800 m to near 1500 m in the interior.

Anyone who has not been exposed to the sheer horror of well developed underbrush, riddled with windfalls, potholes and slippery rocks, interspersed with flourishing patches of stinging nettles and devil's club and swarming with mosquitoes and blackflies, must simply accept that it can drive even well adjusted, mild-tempered adults to screams of rage and tears of frustration and slow progress to tenths of a kilometer per hour!

Think at least twice about taking a direct line through the bush, particularly downhill. While it might look like a shortcut, it could be never-ending. The bush most likely will get thicker on the way down and retreat more difficult. It is quite fesible to follow a compass bearing through the timber in many areas, but it is important to find out ahead of time where that applies. Often that is more easily said than done.

Many of the available topographical maps are quite inadequate for wilderness travel. Only in recent years have 1:50,000 scale maps with either 100 ft. or 20 m contour lines come close to covering the whole of this area. While they are a great improvement on 1:250,000 scale maps with 500 ft. or 150 m contour lines, they show only a few of the existing mining and logging roads and almost none of the trails. In that respect, old editions of large scale maps are superior. Such maps as were produced in the 1920s and 1930s, were based on information gathered by ground survey parties. They used existing trails for access and also surveyed them.

Fortunately, many trails and roads do exist that make access to prime alpine areas a practical proposition, even for families with young children. Most of the trails were built a long time ago with government assistance to encourage prospecting and mineral exploration. Some were so well laid out and constructed that they are still in remarkably good condition after years of neglect. Others have been maintained for various reasons, to the extent that they have weathered the onslaught of undergrowth and erosion. Unfortunately, a lot of the old trails have not fared so well and have largely disappeared. That is a very real loss, not only of the money and labour invested in the original construction, but of an important part of the local history. A real effort has to be made to restore those trails that can still be saved and to maintain those that have remained in good condition. They deserve a better fate than to be forgotten and neglected, particularly in this area where trails are all-important access routes to alpine country. Another consideration is that while resources can sometimes be found for maintenance and restoration projects, our affluent and advanced society would probably be hard put to assemble the skills and resources to construct new trails of the same quality.

Newcomers and visitors from farther south will almost certainly notice the long hours of daylight in the summer. At this latitude there is a surplus of daylight during most of the hiking season. After the end of August, however, the days get noticeably shorter. From then until early March, it is important to keep in mind the number of daylight hours available when outings are planned. Not only are the days short, it is also a poor time of year to be caught out in the dark.

Such factors as snow cover, latitude and climate combine to limit the time when conditions are acceptable for wilderness travel. Also, good conditions tend to occur unpredictably throughout the year and for only short intervals between the passage of Pacific disturbances. Thus, there are no well defined good or bad seasons. To reach the starting point for any outing, it may be necessary to drive a 100 km or more, therefore, the pressure of time is usually a factor and a severe test of organizational and planning ability. It certainly discourages random exploration and the search for access routes. After all, who wants to run the risk of wasting what may well be one of only a few good weekends on a potentially fruitless search?

For those interested in mountaineering, a climber's guide to the entire Coast Range was published by the Alpine Club of Canada in 1968, with a supplement added in a 1969 edition (2). It provides a great deal of additional information of specific interest to mountain climbers, but only sketchy information on access routes.

CLOTHING AND EQUIPMENT

The choice of clothing and equipment is mostly a matter of personal preferences, previous experience and the kind of outing being considered. The bewildering variety of items available often makes the selection process quite difficult. It is not the intention here to go into details, but rather to focus on some fundamental considerations. Numerous books are now available that provide more complete and detailed information. Much has also been written about the skills and knowledge required to make wilderness experiences safe and rewarding. Various organizations arrange courses on every imaginable topic related to wilderness survival. There is much to learn and a lifetime is not enough to find it all out through personal experience, therefore it makes sense to utilize all available sources of information to add to your knowledge and keep it up-to-date.

FOOTWEAR

After what has been said about the geography and climate, it should be obvious that to enjoy the wilderness in this area safely and in reasonable comfort, it is necessary to pay particular attention to clothing and equipment.

It seems logical to put footwear first on the list when dealing with clothing since the feet are all-important to progress. Boots must be comfortable and sturdy, keep the feet dry and provide adequate support and traction. Only high- or medium-cut, good quality leather boots with a vibram-type, rubber sole can do all that. They must be large enough for two pairs of wool socks, but no larger. There is no way around spending a fair amount of money on boots and they must be well looked after. Children also should be outfitted with proper boots and not left to wear runners or rubber boots. Always carry spare, dry socks since wet feet eventually lead to sore feet. Even if the boots get wet, dry, wool socks will help. That really holds only for unlined boots. Lined boots have the additional disadvantage that once they get wet, something that is bound to happen eventually, they take forever to dry.

Footwear for ski touring is not really much different. What is different are the consequences of sore, wet or cold feet. In winter, such problems may become very serious unless something is done about them right away.

CLOTHING

There are two basic principles that should be observed. One is to wear several layers of loose-fitting clothing rather than one or two thick garments. The other is to always wear or carry a windproof outer garment. Adjust the amount of clothing actually worn to match the degree of exertion and to maintain a comfortable body temperature. Avoid getting overheated and sweaty when climbing hard or moving fast. Depending on the particular material, clothes lose some or all their insulating value when wet and it is not always possible to get them dry again. Put clothes on when moving slowly or resting to avoid cooling off too fast or too much.

Maintaining a comfortable body temperature is even more important, but also more difficult in the winter. However, it can get very cold and windy at higher elevations in the summer also. Bad enough that someone who at the same time is wet and exhausted, can be in serious trouble. Therefore, winter and summer, always bring along spare, warm clothing, including a wool hat and mitts.

Shorts and short-sleeved shirts are best avoided. On the rare occasions when weather conditions are suitable, the mosquitoes and blackflies are also likely to be out in force. Various kinds of prickly vegetation and rough terrain likewise tend to discourage such outfits.

Rainwear is always a problem. Anything truly rainproof is usually rubberized or so closely woven that it does not breathe, so if you avoid getting wet from the outside, you get wet from condensation inside. For light rain showers, a good windproof garment is typically also sufficiently waterproof. In heavy, continuous rain, it is practically impossible to remain dry if it is necessary to keep moving. The combined effect of rain and wet bush is unbeatable, so either wait in a dry place for conditions to improve or keep going anyway until it becomes possible to change or dry out. To run out of options at the wrong time and the wrong place, is the real danger. Being soaking wet, cold and unable to move because of exhaustion, injury or technical difficulties is a situation when more options are urgently needed. Having the proper equipment at hand then becomes very important.

EQUIPMENT

The most vital item of equipment is an adequate supply of matches in a waterproof container. In most cases when it is necessary to stop for any length of time, a fire adds greatly to your comfort and well-being. Under adverse conditions, it may be an absolute necessity. Even at the higher elevations, it is unusual to have to move very far down to find fuel. It helps to carry some paper or other fire-starting material. A good knife is fairly essential, not only for gathering fuel, but for many other tasks.

Next in order of importance is probably navigational equipment and a good knowledge of how to use it. Always carry topographical maps covering the area of interest. For reasonably detailed information about the terrain, 1:50,000 (1 cm = 1/2 km) maps with 100 ft. or 20 m contour intervals are best, but to better appreciate the general lie of the land and for taking long range bearings, 1:250,000 (1 cm = 2.5 km) maps with 500 ft. or 150 m contour intervals should also be carried. Some areas are covered by large scale, aerial photographs. They are impractical and too expensive for general use, but invaluable for very precise route finding, particularly when viewed as stereo pairs so the vertical relief shows up.

It is important to spend enough time studying the maps to get a good feel for the lie of the land, e.g. drainage patterns, prominent features, distances, grades etc.. There are two good reasons for that. Distance plus the amount of up and down, provides a fair indication of the time and effort likely to be required en route. It also makes it more difficult to get really lost. With the many prominent and easily identified topographical features so characteristic of this area, it is usually not too much of a problem to determine your location in the field quite closely.

By using either the sun and a watch, or the stars, to find directions, it is possible to get along without a compass. On the other hand, a serviceable compass is light and not unduly expensive and may be very necessary if caught in a fog. It should be liquid-filled to have a short settling time. When following a compass bearing, that is important. Needless to say, it is not a good idea to try navigating by map and compass for the first time, under difficult circumstances, out in the field. Practice at home or in familiar surroundings when there is no pressure of time.

An altimeter is a very useful navigational aid. When used intelligently in conjunction with other aids to navigation, it can help greatly to pinpoint or verify locations.

Although the time required to cover a given distance varies enormously depending on the terrain and conditions, a watch can also be useful for navigation. Most physically fit adults will cover 5-6 km per hour on a good, level trail. On a fair trail, without excessively steep grades, 3 km per hour is a typical average speed. Where there is no trail, through open timber or above timberline, provided the grade is not so severe as to require scrambling or technical climbing, allow one hour for a 300 m gain in elevation. On skis, away from set tracks, rates of progress are much the same as for hiking over level terrain or uphill, but a lot faster downhill. Generally speaking, much more ground can be covered on skis in the winter than on foot in the summer, not only because getting down is so much faster, but also because the snow covers up a lot of obstacles, so it is often possible to follow a straight line course.

With children and novices along, progress is much slower. Frequent stops are required to keep children from getting bored and let novices rest. It is helpful to start out with a good idea of how fast your particular group is likely to move. On very demanding hikes or ski tours, it is essential to know the capabilities of everyone in the party.

During the summer, particularly any time before late August, insect repellant must be considered among the essentials in this area. From September on through the winter, while the days are short, a flashlight can sometimes make the difference between getting home the same day or spending an uncomfortable night out. Once above timberline, sunglasses are necessary when there is snow on the ground.

A small first aid kit should always be carried. Equally important is a good knowledge of emergency first aid. It is well worth taking an emergency repair kit for equipment and clothing. It should rarely be needed if you know your equipment and keep it in good repair, but sometimes things break unexpectedly and must be fixed somehow before you can go on.

NOURISHMENT

Food and drink deserve some mention even though the requirements depend greatly on the length of outing, individual taste and so on. Drink is more important to survival than food, but on the other hand, there are few places and occasions in this area when good drinking water is not readily available, so that normally it is not necessary to carry it. To carry bottles or cans of juice, pop and beer is a total waste of energy. The contents are mostly water in any case, and the empty containers have to be carried out. Hot drinks are very thirst-quenching even on warm, summer days and are a source of quick energy. Probably hot tea is best and , in spite of the extra weight, winter or summer, it is a good idea to carry some in a thermos. It is also possible of course to carry a saucepan or kettle and make tea on the spot, but that takes time and there is no real saving in weight.

On very strenuous trips, particularly in hot weather, a lot of salt is lost from the body. Some people are very sensitive to loss of salt and develop severe muscle cramps. It helps to bring salt along and mix it with any drink to the extent that the tastebuds allow.

When deciding what to take in the way of food, always look for the best ratio of nutritional value to weight. With water being readily available, bring dehydrated foods when possible. It is not difficult to find these days and it does not need to be special purpose, expensive food. Take food that requires little or no preparation. That conflicts somewhat with using dehydrated foods, but the requirements are not altogether incompatible. It certainly makes no sense to bring food that takes hours to prepare and requires dozens of pots and pans. The principle remains the same for anything that has to be carried, maximum utility and minimum weight.

BACKPACKS

No matter how careful the selection, some things must be carried and the weight and volume add up. Obviously it is neseccary to find a backpack that will take it all and be as comfortable as possible. Light-weight packs of all sizes and shapes are now readily available. It is quite impossible to be specific about which is best. Beyond the most basic requirements that it must feel comfortable and provide the optimum combination of weight, size and strength, choose a pack that suits the intended use and fits the budget. Day packs need not be particularly strong, elaborate or expensive. However, for overnight backpacking trips, a pack must be light-weight, strong and comfortable when fully loaded. That combination of qualities puts the price up. For ski touring, a well fitting, comfortable pack is particularly important to make the downhill parts of the trip enjoyable. Skiers who never fall need not worry if the pack is quick and easy to get off or not, but for most, that is an important consideration. Any pack that is so constructed that it will attack you from behind and either knock you out or strangle you in a forward fall, should definitely be avoided!

SKIS

For touring in alpine areas, off maintained trails and in rough terrain, skis must be strong enough and so attached that good control is possible in difficult snow conditions. That effectively rules out specialized, lightweight cross-country skis, bindings and boots. They are well suited to the conditions they are intended for, but not for the mountains, deep snow and rough terrain. For that kind of skiing, use skis that are as wide and as long as you can comfortably handle. They should have metal edges and cable-type bindings that allow enough freedom to lift the heel, but at the same time give good lateral control. If the binding has a safety release, check frequently that it is properly adjusted and be sure to have a safety strap attached. A ski that comes off and escapes down the mountain could leave you stranded in difficult circumstances.

Always carry an emergency ski tip. If a ski breaks, it is almost invariably the tip that goes and few things are less functional than a ski without a tip. A spare binding cable is also essential. With continual flexing, cables do eventually break, invariably when it is least convenient.

Modern ski waxes are extremely good, but in variable snow conditions, it is sometimes difficult to find the right wax. With a heavy pack and much uphill ahead, climbing skins are sometimes the best solution.

FIREARMS

Because of bears, many people would hesitate to go anywhere in this area without a gun of some kind. Bears are indeed large, powerful animals and are abundant throughout West Central British Columbia. Black bears are much more likely to be seen than grizzlies, not only because there are more of them, but also they are nowhere near as shy of people as grizzlies are. However, the chance of meeting either when out hiking is small and the risk of being attacked is very remote.

Like all animals in the wild, bears are cautious and normally inclined to avoid a confrontation with any creature as large as man, if they have a choice. Near built-up areas, bears may have become familiar with people and therefore less cautious and potentially more aggressive.

To be safe, it is necessary to know something about bear behaviour and avoid doing anything they are likely to consider provocative. At best, a firearm adds a narrow margin of safety, but unless expertly handled, it is more likely to do the opposite. Apart from that, a firearm is not only a nuisance to carry on a hike, but is in itself a significant hazard. On balance, it generally makes no sense to take a gun on a hike. It certainly is infinitely safer to roam around in the wilderness without one than it is to drive on any highway or go for a walk in any big city after dark.

LIVE AND LET LIVE!

This book is intended as a helping hand extended to you who wish to experience and enjoy our magnificent wilderness. In return, you are asked to respect and preserve that wilderness and all its trees, plants and creatures. It is a priceless heritage that we all have a right to enjoy, but only on condition that we do nothing to detract from the enjoyment of those who follow. The simple rule, live and let live, sums up what our attitude must be. As is so often the case with simple rules, it is not always easy to live by, but the closer we can come to that, the more enjoyable and satisfying will be the wilderness experience of others who pass the same way.

To live means, among other things, taking full advantage of all opportunities to exercise common sense and judgement. When it comes to caring for the environment, common sense makes it clear that in heavily used or particularly sensitive areas, much greater care is required than in areas that are seldom visited. Most of the high country in this part of the Province still falls into the latter category. That means we can usually permit ourselves the luxury of campfires for cooking and sheer enjoyment; our children can wade through the lush alpine meadows and pick flowers; we do not have to stay on designated trails and we can choose places to camp that we like.

We can only retain the priviledge of governing our own behaviour by common sense if we are prepared to impose greater restrictions on our activities in situations that demand it. As some areas become more heavily used, the disruptions caused by man become greater than nature can cope with. We must respond by not gathering fuel and lighting fires, but instead use stoves. We must concede that walking and camping at will in such areas is no longer acceptable, that picking flowers cannot be permitted and that every scrap of garbage must be carried out.

Anywhere and at all times, there are some things that must be avoided. Never discard glass, plastic, metal and other "everlasting" garbage, pack it out. Never operate snowmobiles, motorbikes or other off-road vehicles so as to disturb wildlife. Off the roads, particularly in alpine areas, tracks left by vehicles scar the terrain for years or even decades, so drive on roads only. Most trails are not built to stand up to use by motorbikes and the like, so keep to roads or specially constructed bike trails. Horses and mountain bikes can make a big mess of trail sections that are soft and wet. Even a steady procession of hiking boots can cause damage, so it is best to stay off soft trail sections until they harden, normally late in the summer.

Apart from the physical impact caused by vehicles of all kinds, there are real conflicts between motorized and other users of the wilderness. Conflicts of that nature are inevitable when people bring an almost infinite variety of demands, pressures and expectations to bear on on a finite, shared resource. Not too long ago, the losers could always flee to more remote areas and live happily until "progress" once again caught up with them. Now it has caught up almost everywhere and we are forced to start solving problems rather than running away from them.

Resource use problems and conflicts can only be resolved or at least managed intelligently when we have an education system that is equal to the task of instilling, in the majority of students, a genuine love, respect and understanding of the wilderness. At the same time, it must bring about an understanding that trade-offs, compromises and risks can never be avoided in real life. The price to be paid eventually for insisting on steadily improving or even preserving our material standard of living, is destruction of the environment. On the other hand, we cannot exist, any more than other species, without exploiting to some degree the available resources.

It is also necessary that our social system and political institutions develop the maturity, sophistication and mechanisms required to facilitate conflict resolution and compromise rather than provoke confrontation and generate a cacophony of single-issue groupings and one-dimensional individuals, intent on fighting their countless holy wars to the bitter end.

It is our misfortune that resource management has evolved in ways that makes the process both illogical and ineffective. Since the land base is common to all resource use activities, such as logging, mining, trapping and outdoor recreation, it makes little sense to have a variety of single-resource oriented agencies managing parcels of land to their own best advantage and with scant regard for the needs of other users. It should be a unified, area based system, with a single agency responsible for management of all resources within its area boundaries. The mandate of each such agency would be to make land use and resource management decisions within the framework of national and provincial legislation and long range policies, but strongly influenced by local objectives. Also, the resource management process should be inverted to make it mandatory that all unexploited crown land be maintained in its natural state, in a land bank. From that bank it would be possible to withdraw land for specific uses, but only after careful consideration, with public input and in accordance with established regulations. Such withdrawals would have to provide the optimum, long range economic returns to the local area, as well as to the Province. Options foregone as a result of withdrawals would have to be evaluated in the process. Instead, we have thrown the entire land base open to exploitation and struggle to set aside, on an ad hoc basis, small areas for preservation as wilderness, parks and reserves. It is a poor substitute for effective management of the whole.

Many people find it hard to understand that the same mountains and wilderness areas we so often refer to as "rugged", "unchanging", "everlasting" and so on, are in fact so fragile. For that to be understood, it must be realized that the growing and rearing season in alpine areas is very short. Flowering plants that carpet the lovely meadows have to reach the seed stage within a brief period, maybe a couple of months at best. Woody plants grow only by minute amounts even in good summers. Years may pass between summers that permit seeds to germinate and new plants to become established.

That sparse, struggling vegetation is what sustains animal life in the high country. It takes a large area to support a single animal. The very existence of animals in what is essentially a harsh and hostile environment, depends on a precarious balance between many complex factors. It takes so little to destroy that balance and so long to repair the damage. Where traffic is heavy enough to destroy plants and roots that bind the soil, erosion quickly follows. To re-establish stability may take many decades. Heavily used trails are sometimes visible for a century after they were last used. Vegetation is also easily smothered by garbage such as cans, bottles, plastic and even paper. A tent left standing in the same place for more than a few days, leaves a permanent scar.

Even those concerned about the environment often find it difficult to accept that they have a part to play in caring for it when they see the appalling mess left behind by activities such as mineral exploration, mining and logging. It is particularly annoying when some resource managers appear to take great delight in insisting that recreationists observe every bureaucratic regulation to the letter and at the same time seem inclined to overlook the most damaging practices by industry. What must be remembered is that the bureaucrats are simply doing as instructed by the politicians, who long ago ceased to be leaders and just follow where the polls lead. So long as we act and vote in ways that makes it clear we place the highest priority on material possessions, then no matter what we say, government and industry will carry on with no regard for future generations. In the final analysis, their actions and attitudes simply reflect the desires and outlook of the general public. Only when we recognize and acknowledge that as the problem, can we have any real hope of starting the long climb back up the slippery slope we are on.

Skiers and snowmobilers have much to gain from co-operating.

KITIMAT-TERRACE AREA

This section deals with the southwest corner of the West Central British Columbia region and covers an area of roughly 50 by 80 km, south of the Skeena and Zymoetz Rivers and west of Clore River.

There are relatively few good access routes right to timberline, although many logging roads lead to within striking distance of some rugged and spectacular alpine areas. The problem is that to reach them usually involves at least a couple of hours of bush-whacking up some very steep, rough slopes. There are a few good trails accessible from Hwy.37 between Kitimat and Terrace and farther east, a logging road extends up Clore River. It makes it possible, but not easy to approach some very impressive peaks that are somewhat hidden and not readily apparent from the highway.

Best known of the mountains in the area are Mt. Elizabeth, less than 2000 m, but providing an impressive and pleasing backdrop for the town of Kitimat, and Thornhill Mountain, overlooking Terrace.

GEOGRAPHICAL FEATURES

The dominant peaks along the eastern boundary closely define the spine of the Coast Range mountains. Several are well over 2000 m with Andesite Peak at 2380 m being the highest. Since the southwest boundary follows the coastline, it means that the total vertical relief is nearly 2400 m, however, it would be difficult to find a vantage point from which to observe that. Generally, elevations increase more or less uniformly from west to east, so the lower peaks in the foreground dominate and obscure the higher, distant peaks.

With the exception of the major north-south valley between Kitimat and Terrace, most of the valleys run more or less east-west. They are mostly deep, steep-sided and densely forested. The undergrowth in the bottom-land is typically so thick as to be virtually impenetrable. Rivers and streams are fast-flowing and cold. Where they are not roaring through narrow canyons and over waterfalls, they tend to meander all over flat, marshy valley bottoms. Timberline is generally close to 1000 m. Below that level, hemlock, cedar and balsam predominate.

The combination of precipitous terrain, dense underbrush and cold, rushing streams makes it frustrating, time consuming and to a degree hazardous to embark on a direct line through the bush. Thus the valleys offer very little encouragement as access routes in the absence of roads or trails.

The climate is uncompromisingly coastal: temperatures are generally moderate, but precipitation is heavy - up to 300 mm per year. Much of it comes as snow, so heavy snowfalls are not uncommon during the winter. Moving away from the coast towards the north and east, there is a significant drop in precipitation even within this relatively small area, with Terrace getting about half as much as Kitimat. The most disconcerting aspects of the

17

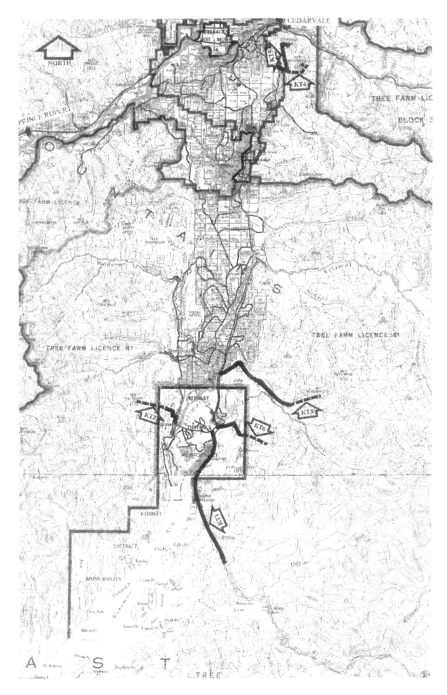

# KITIMAT-TERRACE AREA
1cm=5km, 150m contour interval

18

climate are unpredictability and rapid change. It is impossible to define any particular season as dry, since it may be dry one year and more than likely wet the next.

An interesting and unique topographical feature is the great trench, 6 to 8 km wide in places, extending from the Nass River in the north to tidewater at the head of Kitimat Arm in the south. It is occupied in turn by the Tseax, Kitsumkalum, Lakelse and Kitimat Rivers and is in complete contrast to the deep, narrow valleys and fiords so characteristic of the west coast. The origin of the trench is still the subject of debate. R.G. McConnell in a 1912 report (3) and G. Hanson in 1922 and 1923 geolgical survey reports (4,5) speculate that this great valley, now occupied by relatively small streams, once carried the waters of the Nass, joined by the Skeena at Terrace, to the sea at Kitimat. A. Gottesfeld (1) associates it with a Kitimat/Kalum Valley fault system co-inciding with the boundary between the Stikine Terrane and the Coast Plu-tonic Complex. As such, it also helps to explain the occurrence of hotsprings at Lakelse Lake and several smaller ones along Douglas Channel, as well as the quite recent Tseax lava flow, just south of the Nass.

The contact zone between the Coast Range granites and the older, in-terior volcanic and sedimentary rocks is also interesting because of the min-eralization that has occurred there. It has led to significant exploration and some mining activity in the area, resulting in the construction of some access trails to the high country above timberline that are still useable.

In an area so dominated by dense, coastal forests, much rain and even more snow, there are relatively few moose and deer. However, recent clear-cutting of large blocks of timber, together with a long succession of low snow-fall years, has resulted in a greater number of such animals. Rich berry crops and large runs of spawning salmon, provide a feast for the numerous black bears and occasional grizzly. Above timberline, the rugged, inaccessible ter-rain is a haven for a healthy population of mountain goats.

HISTORICAL NOTES

G. Robinson has done much to document the history of the purely Ind-ian era, prior to the beginning of this century (6,7,8). He relates that the first white man to arrive and stay for any length of time in Kitimat was a lay min-ister who came in 1878. Others followed and in 1891, G.L. Anderson came to homestead on the flats at the mouth of Kitimat River. It is his name that is perpetuated in Anderson Creek. A book (9) written by his daughter, Eliza-beth Anderson Varley, was published in 1981 and contains much fascinating information about the life of the early, white settlers in the Kitimat Valley. She will also be be well remembered by the lovely mountain that bears her name and overlooks Kitimat.

Some of the background to white settlement in the Kitimat Valley and plans for the area can be found in a 1913 Department of Lands publication (10). The land around Kitimat had been placed in a reserve in 1898 and later subdivided into 40 acre lots, open to pre-emtion in the fall of 1913. The year

1898 is significant because by then there was talk of a Pacific Northern & Omenica Railway that would link Kitimat with the interior via Telkwa Pass. In anticipation of development, waterfront land was purchased that same year by C.W.D. Clifford, MLA for Skeena and one of the principal promoters of the rail link. The Province granted a charter to the Kitimat-Omenica railway in 1900. A $5000/mile subsidy for construction was provided, contingent on the Company spending $100,000 by 1905. Clifford built a hotel and store as well as a wharf on lot #89, the same now occupied by Alcan's wharf.

Prospectors started to show up in the area just prior to the year 1900. Isolated claims were staked in various locations with ready access to tidewater. One of the earliest was the Golden Crown group of claims on Wahugh (now Wathl) Creek, about 7 km east of Kitamaat Village, staked prior to 1900 by Steel and Dunn. In 1901, a wagon road to the claims was built with government assistance. The property had fairly good surface showings of gold and copper ore, but was abandoned in 1909 after considerable exploratory work had failed to disclose any significant ore bodies.

In the years 1904-1906, Kitimat experienced something of a boom as a result of railway fever. There was quite an influx of settlers, speculators and people travelling through to the interior over the trail to Terrace. This was an old Indian trail from Kitimat to the Skeena, widened and improved during the summer of 1898 to accommodate dog teams for the winter mail run to communities on the upper Skeena. Previously the mail had been taken up the Skeena from Port Essington over the ice, a long and dangerous journey.

When in 1912, Prince Rupert was chosen as the western terminus of the railway, Kitimat entered a period of decline. The wharf collapsed and Anderson eventually dismantled the hotel. During World War I, most of the remaining settlers left. Of the few who returned after the war, Charles Moore remained in Kitimat until he died in 1943. He was the last of the old-timers to go. It was his name that was given to the creek that now bisects the Alcan smelter.

Discovery of the hotsprings at Lakelse Lake is attributed to one of the early travellers, a man named M.C. Kendal, who came across them in 1894. Obviously the Indians knew about them much earlier. In her book (11) about the history of Terrace, Asante states that there was once a large Indian community at Lakelse Lake, but that it was abandoned before the turn of the century. The 1914 Minister of Mines annual report makes reference to some superstition that is said to have caused Indians to avoid the area.

The Lakelse hotsprings were acquired by H.N. Boss and J.B. Johnstone in 1907 and in 1910 they put up log building to serve as a hotel and bathhouse. It was a two storey affair with 14 bedrooms for which they charged $4 per day. They had cattle and a vegetable garden. Access was by wagon road from Terrace to the lake and the rest of the way by boat. From May to October every year, business was apparently good. A new and larger hotel was built in 1929, but was closed in 1936 as a result of the depression (8).

A water analysis given in the 1914 Minister of Mines annual report shows a total mineral content of 83 grains per gallon, consisting mainly of lime with some soda and magnesium in the form of chlorides and sulphates. No potash or lithia was found to be present. The hotsprings is actually a group of 13 springs with the total flow reported to be over 300,000 gallons per day, with the largest spring more than 100 ft. in diameter and contributing just over one third of that total. The water temperature was recorded as 180 degrees Fahrenheit.

In view of current concerns about declining salmon stocks, it is interesting to note that it was a matter of concern as long ago as the end of the last century. As a result, several hatcheries were constructed on creeks flowing into Lakelse Lake. The first one went into operation in 1901 and the last one was shut down in 1936 (11).

The origins of Alcan's smelter and modern Kitimat can be traced back to 1928, when provincial surveyors saw the possibility of damming the eastward flow of a series of interior lakes and diverting the water through a tunnel to a hydro-electric power station on tidewater. Alcan was approached as one of the few companies that might be able to utilize the vast amount of energy avilable from such a scheme. However, at the time there was not sufficient interest or capital to go ahead and eventually World War II intervened. After the war, interest in the scheme revived and in 1948 Alcan took the momentous decision to go ahead with the project. Construction started in 1951 and in 1954 the first aluminum was produced. A railway to Kitimat at long last became a reality and by 1957, Kitimat was connected by Hwy.37 (then Hwy.25) to the rest of the Province. The complete story of Alcan's Kemano-Kitimat project, from its conception over 60 years ago to the present, has been related in fascinating detail and most readably in a recent book (12) by John Kendrick, who was intimately involved with the unfolding saga right from day one.

Smelters, such as Alcan's, utilizing only locally generated electrical energy, may be as close to a mining industry as the Kitimat-Terrace area will ever get. The geology does not generally favour large-scale mineralization, so that compared with other parts of West Central British Columbia, relatively little exploration and mining activity has taken place. That is not to say the ground has not been quite thoroughly gone over by prospectors. Apart from the Golden Crown claims already mentioned, claims were staked in 1928 at the head of Kildala Arm, in an area considered favourable to possible copper deposits. Other claims were staked at the head of Minette Bay. Farther up the valley, Iron Mountain was also the site of exploration activity starting in about 1908 and continuing into the 1920's.

An exception to the general pattern is Thornhill Mountain and the entire ridge system forming the divide between Zymoetz River and Williams Creek. There, volcanic and sedimentary rock formations related to those of Kitselas Mountain, on the opposite side of the Skeena, are in evidence. Numerous claims in the area are repeatedly referred to in Minister of Mines annual reports over the 20-year period between 1910 and 1930. Evidently,

21

Looking west over Kitimat from Robinson Ridge.

Kitimat's Mt. Elizabeth.

some of those claims showed promising values of gold, silver and copper, with some molybdenite occurring towards the south end of the ridge.

On the ridge south of Williams Creek, only one area seems to have warranted serious exploration. That was the location of the Copper Queen group of claims. It was reached by following a good horse trail up Williams Creek for about 8 km to Bell's cabin and then crossing to the south side of the creek. From there, the trail climbed steeply on switchbacks for 5 km to timberline at 1000 m. The claims were still a few kilometers farther along through the meadows. In 1922 and again in 1930, The Department of Mines contributed funds to assist with trail construction. A trail also continued up Williams Creek. The 1930 Minister of Mines annual report mentions that on the divide between Williams Creek and Trapline Creek there are some fine clay deposits. Unfortunately, those trails, beyond the point where the present logging road up Williams Creek crosses the creek and diverges to the south, are now in such a poor state that a major clearing effort would be required to make them usable again.

FUTURE PROSPECTS

The Kitimat-Terrace corridor, with exceptionally good access to tide-water and the wide, pleasant valleys occupied by the Kitimat and Lakelse Rivers, has great potential for considerable industrial development and population growth in the foreseeable future. The same, large area of flat valley-bottom land is also ideally suited for growing trees. Intensive, highly mechanized silvicultural and harvesting methods could be employed to yield superior timber values much more rapidly than is possible elsewhere on the North Coast. Thus, the potential for conflict is also great, as is so often the case in British Columbia, where good valley-bottom land is a scarce commodity.

While the climate leaves something to be desired from the point of view of outdoor recreationists and many will want to travel farther inland to go hiking and skiing, that is not always the case. When the weather is good, the local scenery and recreational opportunities compare favourably with what is available elsewhere. Some activities, such as salt water boating and fishing, are simply not available at all anywhere else. Lakelse Lake also is a unique recreational resource. Not only does it have the hotsprings, but it is the only large body of fresh water that warms up enough in the summer for swimming and similar water sports.

The increasing pressure on all outdoor recreational resources in the area has become noticeable in recent years. Much has been done to improve the opportunities and spread the load. Construction of a trail up Mt.Eliza-beth is a good example, as is the trail to Robinson Ridge and the cabin put up there. More initiatives like that are needed to encourage not only local hikers and skiers, but to attract tourists and so diversify the local economy.

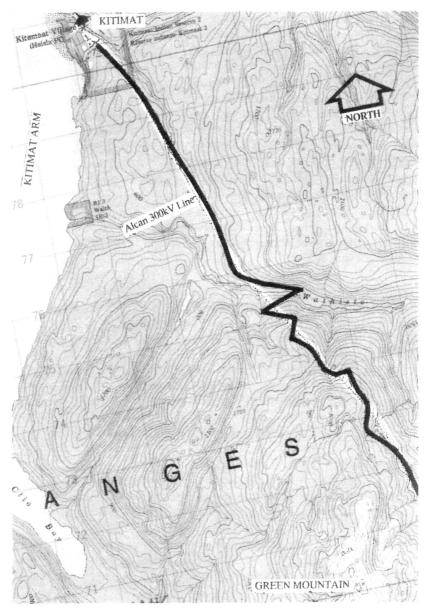

GREEN MOUNTAIN ROAD [KT1]

(Part of Map 103H/15)

1cm=2/3km, 100ft.(30m) contour interval

GREEN MOUNTAIN ROAD [KT1]

LOCATION:
Kitimat-Terrace area, near Kitimat.

MAPS REQUIRED:
103I/2 Kitimat (1:50,000)
103H/15 Kitimat Arm (1:50,000)
103H Douglas Channel (1:250,000)

DIRECTIONS:
Heading north out of Kitimat on Haisla (Hwy.37) and opposite the intersection with Nalabila, turn right onto the road signed "MK Bay Marina 11 km". Follow the road past the marina entrance and shortly thereafter cross Wathl Creek. Where the road turns sharp right to enter Kitamaat Village, Green Mountain Road continues straight ahead up the hill. Near the base of the hill is a locked gate with an Alcan sign. The road is owned and maintained by the Aluminum Company of Canada (Alcan Smelters and Chemicals) and is used to service the transmission line crossing over Green Mountain on its way to Kitimat from the generating station at Kemano some 80 km to the south. The Company will not normally permit private vehicles on the road, but makes no attempt to hinder pedestrian access.

COMMENTS:
Except for a short, steep climb immediately after the gate, there is no significant change in elevation for the first 7 km or so. The road then crosses Wathlsto Creek and climbs quite steeply for the next 3 km to about 850 m. After that it remains more or less level for the next 4 - 5 km before it starts to drop down again towards Kildala Arm. At its highest point, the road comes close to timberline, which is between 800 and 900 m so near the coast.

The view from the 1200 m summit of Green Mountain, just west of the road, out over Kitimat Arm and Douglas and Devastation Channels is quite spectacular. From the 1400 m Haisla Mountain, east of the road, there is a fine view of Atna Peak which towers to 2750 m about 30 km to the east.

A good time of the year to go up Green Mountain is late winter when under favourable snow conditions, the somewhat tedious road can be covered reasonably quickly on skis. Skiing is good through the sparse timber to both the east and the west summits. The run back down the road is exhilarating for competent skiers, but it is important to keep some energy in reserve for the last 7 km on the flat.

With the advent of mountain bikes, going up the road in the summer has become a much more interesting proposition. The ride down is rough and steep, but it saves a great deal of time and energy when compared with walking and the long, flat section is nowhere near as tedious.

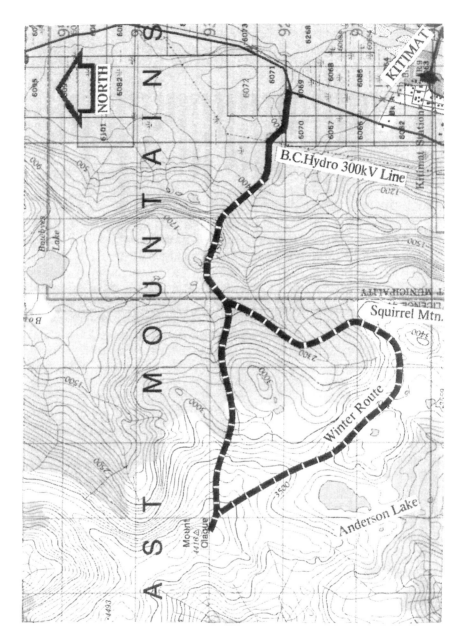

CLAGUE MOUNTAIN TRAIL [KT2]

(Part of Map 103I/2)

1cm=1/2km, 100ft.(30m) contour interval

CLAGUE MOUNTAIN TRAIL [KT2]

LOCATION:
Kitimat-Terrace area, near Kitimat.

MAPS REQUIRED:
103I/2 Kitimat (1:50,000)
103I Terrace (1:250,000)

ROUTE DESCRIPTION:
About 5 km from start of trail 100 m above sea level to the summit of Clague at elevation 1350 m. A well defined trail all the way, but very muddy in places. The first 2 km or so is a "cat" road put in to access mineral claims. At the start, the road switchbacks up an area cleared in the early days of Kitimat as a ski hill, but never used. The slashing is quite steep with an elevation gain of 300 m in less than 1 km. After that, the road flattens out briefly before climbing steeply again. The terrain then slopes up more gently and at the top of the slope, elevation approximately 600 m, the road ends in a small valley running more or less north-south.

A trail continues up the steep hill across the valley to the west. At the top, it crosses a small creek and emerges into an open, gently sloping valley at elevation 800 m, which is timberline near the coast. Thereafter, the trail gradually climbs onto the ridge on the right (north) and follows it to the summit. A second summit close to 2 km distant in a northwesterly direction is actually higher by about 40 m.

There is an easier, more pleasant, but longer, winter route up the valley in a southerly direction from the end of the "cat" road. Follow the valley for 1 km or so and then climb out onto the ridge on the left (south). The east end of that ridge is known locally as Squirrel Mountain. Alternatively, continue up the valley for another kilometer and climb out on the north side. Either route goes steeply up through fairly open timber that poses no serious problem for experienced skiers on the way down. Both give good access to the main, southeasterly ridge that leads to the summit of Clague Mountain.

Allow 3-4 hours to the summit from the start of the trail ("cat" road) and about 2 hours down. In the winter, so much depends on snow conditions that the time required could vary from about the same as in summer to more than double.

DIRECTIONS:
Drive south on Hwy.37 (Haisla) across the bridge over Kitimat River, but where the main road turns left, continue straight ahead on Station and then turn right onto Enterprise Avenue. Just beyond the last buildings, there is a sharp turn left after which the road crosses the railway track. At the next cross road, 1 km from the intersection of Station and Enterprise, turn right

Mts. Carthew, Madden and Holt from Clague Mountain.

and follow the main logging road north for just over 1 km, then turn left onto a side road. With a few twists and turns it maintains a generally westerly heading. About 1 km in, it climbs up onto a bench and passes under a power-line and after another kilometer it ends where the trail ("cat" road) starts at the base of the slashed area.

COMMENTS:

This trail provides quick, convenient access to a large alpine area. It is a steep, muddy and somewhat unattractive route for the first couple of kilometers, but beyond that the view opens up and the alpine terrain starts.Once above timberline, a great expanse of good hiking and ski-touring country becomes reasonably accessible.

On skis, the major problem is getting up and down the steep section at the start. Except under very favourable snow conditions, most people will find it easiest to carry their skis both up and down that part.

It is a good idea to pick a day when the wind is from the north to go up Clague Mountain. Not only is the weather most likely to be fair then, but the fumes from the smelter and pulpmill are blown out to sea and so do not detract from an otherwise enjoyable experience.

Young children and even those that are older, but lack hiking/skiing experience, are not likely to find this an enjoyable trail because of the steep, tedious section at the start.

MT. ELIZABETH TRAIL [KT3]

LOCATION:
Kitimat-Terrace area, near Kitimat.

MAPS REQUIRED:
103I/1 Mt.Davies (1:50,000)
103I/2 Kitimat (1:50,000)
103I Terrace (1:250,000)

ROUTE DESCRIPTION:
From start of trail at elevation 500 m to the summit at 1850 m, the distance is about 5 km. At the start there is a short section of trail up a logged off
area after which it switchbacks up through fairly open timber for 2 km or so
until it reaches timberline at elevation 1200 m. It is a good, well defined trail,
uniformly steep all the way to timberline. While it starts off in a northerly direction, the trail gradually turns to the right so that it emerges from the timber
heading due east.

Above the 1200 m level, the trail very gradually turns left again and for
the last kilometer, from the 1750 m summit of Little Elizabeth across to
Mt. Elizabeth, the heading is once more almost due north.

The trail above timberline is a series of steps, alternately very steep and
fairly level. It is well defined and easy to follow when visibility is good.
Essentially, the route is along the spine of the ridge situated immediately
south and east of Elizabeth Creek. Keeping that in mind is important if fog
or low clouds move in to obscure the view. To avoid serious problems on the
way down, take care not to walk off that ridge either to the right or the left.

From Little Elizabeth there is a short, steep drop down into the saddle
that connects the two summits. The main summit is much like a pile of loose
rocks, but going up is easier than it might appear at first sight. Dropping back
down into the saddle requires a little more care.

Allow 4-6 hours to the summit from the trail head and 3-4 hours down.

DIRECTIONS:
From the intersection of Haisla and Nalabila in Kitimat, follow Hwy.37
north for 8 km. There, just before the highway passes under a powerline, a
signpost on the right points to the gravel road leading to Mt. Elizabeth. Follow that main logging road until it eventually approaches and then follows the
north bank of Hirsch Creek upstream. Right after crossing Elizabeth Creek,
14 km from the highway, turn left onto a branch road signed "Mt.Elizabeth
Trail". The elevation at the turn-off is 200 m. After one more kilometer and a
climb to 320 m, another sign points again to a turn-off on the left. Over the
next 1.5 km that branch road makes a semi-circle to the right and climbs to
elevation 500 m where it ends at the marked trail head.

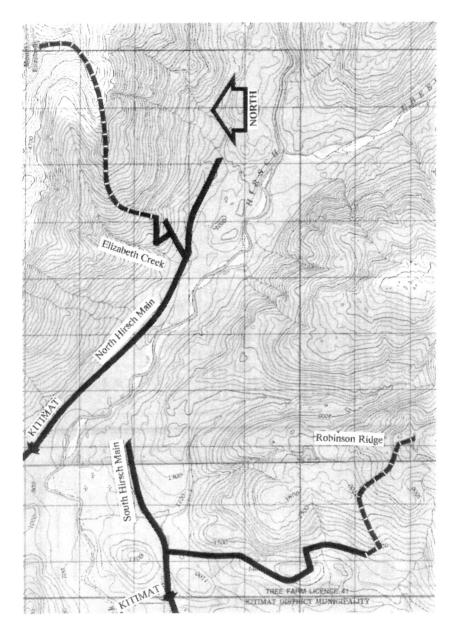

MT. ELIZABETH TRAIL [KT3]
ROBINSON RIDGE TRAIL [KT6]
(Part of Maps 103I/1&2)
1cm=2/3km, 100ft.(30m) contour interval

30

Under favourable conditions, the trail head can be reached by 4-wheel drive vehicle and a standard vehicle can be driven to the turn-off at elevation 320 m where there is space to turn around and park.

COMMENTS:

Mt. Elizabeth presides impressively over Kitimat and is a well known local landmark. In her book "Kitimat My Valley" (9), Elizabeth Anderson Varley relates that during the years when she grew up on the Anderson ranch, near today's Kitimat, she used to refer to it as "My Mountain". As a result, it was eventually named Mt. Elizabeth by Dominion surveyor P.M. Monckton while he was using the ranch as his base during the 1924 season.

In the early days of modern Kitimat it naturally attracted the attention of hikers. In those days and indeed until the late 1960's, when logging roads began to penetrate some distance up Hirsch Creek, it was a mark of some distinction to have been to the top of Mt. Elizabeth. It could only be reached by what eventually became a well worn trail up the south bank of Hirsch Creek. Crossing the creek was always a challenge and after that it was a long, steep hike to get up on the main west ridge and an even longer hike along the ridge to the peak. The ridge appears deceptively smooth from below, but is in fact a seemingly never-ending series of ups and downs. It was usually a matter of three long days to get to the summit and back.

The present route became viable when logging roads on the north side of Hirsch Creek reached Elizabeth Creek. It was first described in a 1975 write-up prepared by Mrs.G. Mendel, then in charge of the Kitimat Museum and an outdoor enthusiast of some renown. After an organized hike in July 1979 that saw 30 people get at least as far as Little Elizabeth, the new route was well established and the following year it was made into a trail under a student work program. If not the first, it was certainly one of the first trails to timberline in West Central British Columbia to be put in solely for recreational purposes. The Mt. Elizabeth Trail has since been designated as Recreation Trail T5 on the Forest Service's Terrace-Nass Recreation Sites map and has been further improved.

The view from the summit out over Kitimat and down the channel is superb and now that it is possible to get up and down in a single day, it is a trip well worth making. The chances of being able to predict what the weather and visibility will be like at the top are much better too, of course.

It is important to be in good physical condition to enjoy the hike because to go up and down close to 1500 m in one day is quite strenuous. Children under 10, and even those who are older, but not used to challenging hikes, are not likely to enjoy going up or down this uncompromisingly steep trail.

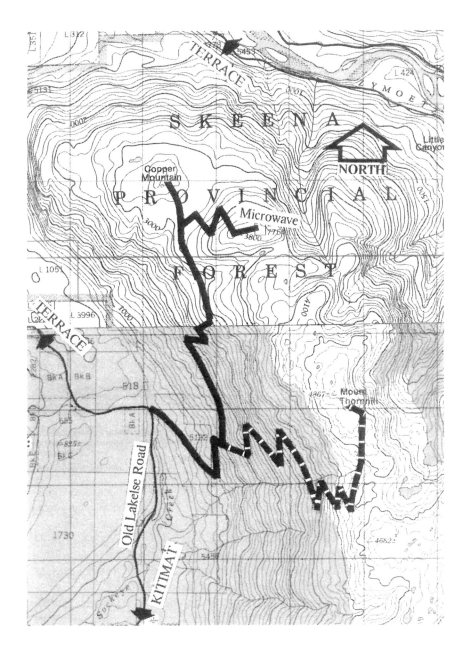

THORNHILL MOUNTAIN TRAIL [KT4]
COPPER MOUNTAIN ROAD [KT5]
(Part of Maps 103I/8&9)
1cm=1/2km, 100ft.(30m) contour interval

THORNHILL MOUNTAIN TRAIL [KT4]

LOCATION:
Kitimat-Terrace area, near Terrace.

MAPS REQUIRED:
103I/8 Chist Creek (1:50,000)
103I/9 Usk (1:50,000)
103I Terrace (1:250,000)

ROUTE DESCRIPTION:
About 5 km from start of trail at elevation 400 m to the 1500 m summit. An excellent trail, well laid out and maintained. It originated as a pack trail serving various mineral claims on the Thornhill Range. For many years it also gave access to a Forestry fire lookout on the summit. The remains of the lookout are still visible.

The mountainside is very steep almost to the top, but with numerous switchbacks, the grade along the trail is fairly easy and remarkably uniform all the way, a tribute to the skills of the prospectors who built the trail.

For the first couple of kilometers through mostly open timber, the trail bears to the right (southerly). Above timberline, near elevation 1200 m, it gradually swings to the left and crosses over the ridge so that it eventually approaches the summit from the south and east.

Allow 3-4 hours up and about 2 hours down.

DIRECTIONS:
From Hwy.16/37 in Thornhill, near Terrace, turn south onto Old Lakelse Road and follow it for just over 6 km. If approaching from Kitimat, turn right off Hwy.37 about 3 km north of Furlong Bay campsite and follow Old Lakelse Road for almost 10 km. At that point take the side road to the east. It immediately bears right to almost parallel Old Lakelse Road for a short distance and then starts to switchback up the hillside. After climbing some 200 m over a distance of about 2 km, and just at a sharp turn left onto a northerly heading, is the signed trailhead. There is just enough space to turn around and park there. Across the road, the trail starts with a scramble up a short, steep section to intersect the original packtrail that is heading southerly.

The road continues on to the top of Copper Mountain [KT5] and serves various radio and TV transmitters and microwave repeaters located there. At least to the start of the Thornhill Mountain Trail, the road is generally good enough for standard vehicles.

COMMEMTS:

There are fine views out over the Kitimat and Skeena valleys from many points along the trail, even quite low down. It offers exceptionally pleasant walking as it winds its way up through big timber that has inhibited undergrowth and erosion. It provides a convincing demonstration of how a trail should be laid out and built to last where the terrain is steep and difficult. From below, it seems like a minor miracle that there is any trail at all up that precipitous mountainside !

At intervals along the trail there is good drinking water. Towards the top where the grade eases off, the trail enters an area of pleasant little meadows and streams where signs of mineral exploration are still visible. From the crest of the ridge, there is a good view of the Zymoetz Valley and the mountains beyond, including the Seven Sisters in the distance. Small lakes fill many of the depressions in the ridge.

From the top of Thornhill Mountain it is a relatively easy hike north to Copper Mountain. Most of the way is downhill, but the last kilometer or so is a steep, uphill scramble where it is best to keep well to the right (east) of the central rock face. The road down from Copper Mountain [KT5] provides an easy route back to the start of Thornhill Mountain Trail. In total, that route down adds 2-3 hours to the return trip time.

Children should enjoy the hike to Thornhill Mountain, both up and down. The trail climbs at a reasonable rate, but steadily enough that elevation is gained quite quickly. There are no significant obstacles to impede progress and waste energy. Best of all, great reserves of energy are not required for the way home: children have lots of fun running down. The view from the top is spectacular enough to even impress most children. It may take a little effort and some imagination on the part of parents to keep children from getting "tired", i.e. bored, and stopping every few minutes lower down on the trail, but perseverance is amply rewarded in this case.

The Forest Service Recreation Map for Terrace-Nass lists this as Recreation Trail T3.

Terrace from

Thornhill Mountain.

COPPER MOUNTAIN ROAD [KT5]
(Route map on p.32)

LOCATION:
Kitimat-Terrace area, near Terrace.

MAPS REQUIRED:
103I/8 Chist Creek (1:50,000)
103I/9 Usk (1:50,000)
103I Terrace (1:250,000)

DIRECTIONS:
Proceed as for Thornhill Mountain Trail [KT4], but instead of stopping at the trail head, keep going up the road. It continues for another 4 or 5 km to two microwave repeater stations at the top, elevation 1200 m. The gate, 1 km or so from the top, at elevation 900 m, may be locked. However, from there it is an easy walk up, mostly above timberline. Just before the gate, there is a side road to the left (west) that in less than a kilometer leads to the Copper Mountain TV and radio transmitter sites at elevation 1000 m.

The road is normally well maintained and standard vehicles can often make it right to the gate, or to the top if the gate is open.

COMMENTS:
Copper Mountain is an isolated outpost at the northwest end of a long ridge seperating Zymoetz River and Williams Creek. To reach the main ridge, it is necessary to drop down 100 m or so into the intervening saddle. That is best accomplished by keeping well over to the Zymoetz River side where a sketchy trail leads down into the saddle. Thornhill Mountain is the next significant summit along the ridge. It is only a couple of kilometers away, but requires a climb up of nearly 500 m from the saddle. Also, the ridge has a lot of ups and downs to impede progress. The best route is not obvious and some care must be taken to avoid wandering off the ridge. From Thornhill Mountain there is a good trail down [KT4].

In summer, when the road is drivable, Copper Mountain Road provides very easy access to alpine areas and some impressive views in all directions: up and down the Skeena, up the Zymoetz and Kitsumkalum valleys and towards Kitimat and Douglas Channel with Lakelse Lake sparkling in the foreground. During the winter, when snow conditions are good, the road offers easy ski access to the entire Thornhill ridge and a pleasant downhill run. However, the road is also a popular snowmobile route, so be cautious when skiing down.

ROBINSON RIDGE TRAIL [KT6]

(Route map on p.30)

LOCATION:
Kitimat-Terrace area, near Kitimat.

MAPS REQUIRED:
103I/1 Mount Davies (1:50,000)
103I/2 Kitimat (1:50,000)
103I Terrace (1:250,000)

ROUTE DESCRIPTION:

From start of trail at elevation 500 m to timberline at 1100 m, it is about 3 km. The trail is well defined, but is primarily a winter trail, so much of it is rough and/or muddy. It starts off in a southeasterly direction, but after crossing a gully, turns gradually to the left until it heads northeasterly up an ill defined lateral ridge. There are some semi-open, marshy steps in the ridge, otherwise this first kilometer of trail climbs steeply through heavy timber. Where the trail intersects the wide main ridge, a small lake and beyond it a large marshy area and, on the far side of the ridge, a bigger lake, occupy a well defined saddle. The trail immediately turns onto a southeasterly heading and follows the main ridge up the rest of the way, again climbing steeply through fairly dense timber. Then, after less than a kilometer, the trees thin out rapidly as the trail heads towards a high point on the ridge. Beyond it, the trail drops down again to a small lake where it ends.

On the far side of the lake is a cabin built jointly by the local snowmobile and cross-country ski clubs. From there, it is easy to follow the open ridge continuing steeply up to terminate as an extensive, rounded summit at elevation 1300 m.

Allow 2-3 hours from start of trail up to the cabin and 1-2 hours down.

DIRECTIONS:

Just north of the intersection of Haisla (Hwy.37) and Nalabila, turn right onto Forest Avenue. Continue on without making any significant change in direction to a fork in the road about 1 km from the highway. Take the road bearing right which is South Hirsch Main. At the fork is km 0. Between km 7 and km 8 turn right onto branch road #100. After a short descent, it climbs quite steeply. In less than a kilometer there is an intersection. Take the road up the hill straight ahead, which is actually branch road #110. Branch road #100 goes to the left and branch #111 to the right. The general heading remains southerly right to the end, which is just over 4 km from the junction with South Hirsch Main. Look for the start of the trail in line with the road. In the summer, all or most of the road is usually passable for standard vehicles, but in the winter, it may be that not even South Hirsch Main is plowed.

Cabin on Robinson Ridge.

COMMENTS:

In winter, there is usually a well packed snowmobile trail as far as the cabin. When that is the case, it is easy for skiers to get up and down on foot while carrying their skis. Without the packed trail, it is only in exceptionally favourable snow conditions that it is a reasonable proposition to ski up and down. The terrain is so steep and heavily timbered that a descent on skis tends to be both undignified and uncontrolled! Under some snow conditions, wearing snowshoes and carrying skis on the way up and down may be the best solution.

Above the cabin, both skiing and hiking are excellent. An extensive ridge system makes a large area easily accessible. However, the topography is quite complex and some of the terrain is steep and rough. It is not a place to go wandering around when the visibility is poor. Map and compass are necessary items of equipment and some knowledge and awareness of avalanche hazards is essential.

Robinson Ridge, located on the east side of Kitimat Valley, is free of air pollution from the pulpmill and smelter no matter which way the wind blows. In that respect it is a more attractive recreation area than Clague Mountain [KT2] on the other side of the valley.

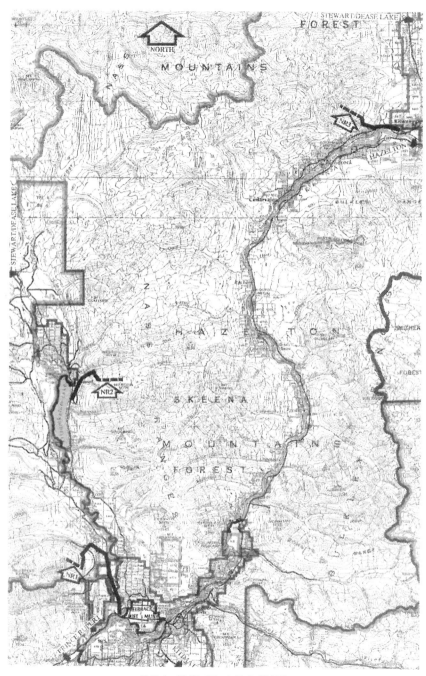

NASS RANGE

1cm=5km, 150m contour interval

38

NASS RANGE

The Nass Range mountains extend north from Terrace for a distance of 120 km. At its widest, the range covers 60 km from Kitwanga in the east to Aiyansh in the west. Only the southern half of the range considered here.

All the major peaks are located on the north-south spine of the range. Most are close to 2000 m in elevation, but taper off at the south end to about 1500 m. It is quite a compact range, visible almost in its entirety from several points in the relatively wide, surrounding valleys. At Terrace, the valley-bottom elevation is less than 100 m, so despite the modest height of the peaks, the Nass Range is impressive.

Extensive logging in Kitsumkalum Valley, up to an elevation of 900 m in some places, for a time provided good access to much of the range from the west. Unfortunately, most of the logging roads were poorly laid out and constructed, so that they have washed out or are overgrown with alder to the extent that they are no longer passable. What is worse, some of the good trails, left as a legacy of extensive prospecting and mineral exploration in the early years of this century, have been obliterated by logging or can no longer be reached.

On the east side of the range, the Skeena blocks access from Hwy.16 and the railway line, on the west side of the Skeena, only marginally facilitates access, since VIA Rail passenger service is so infrequent. A bridge constructed across the Skeena near the mouth of Hardscrabble Creek, to harvest timber west of the river, may or may not improve access to alpine areas on the east side of the Nass Range.

Although it is outside the Nass Range, Sleeping Beaty Trail [NR1], just west of Kitsumkalum River, has been included in this section because it is so closely associated with Terrace.

GEOGRAPHICAL FEATURES

Kisumkalum Valley, the western boundary of the Nass Range, is also generally the eastern line of contact between the Coast Range granites and the interior sedimentary and volcanic series of rocks. The Coast Range is essentially a huge mass of plutonic rock or batholith, 50 to 150 million years old, stretching the length of the Province and into Alaska (13). Bordering the batholith on either side are broad belts of altered volcanic and sedimentary rocks, with unaltered rocks farther away from the contact zone. The whole story of the complex and fascinating geology of the area, can best be understood by reading Gottesfeld's recent book (1) on that subject.

From any point above timberline on the western slopes of the Nass Range, the wide, flat-bottomed Kitsumkalum Valley is an impressive sight. Part of the attraction is Kitsumkalum Lake, but most striking is that the valley appears to continue in an unbroken line to the distant southern horizon.

Another of nature's impressive manifestations, associated with the northward extention of Kitsumkalum Valley, is the massive lava flow, just over the divide towards the Nass River. The flow stretches nearly 25 km from the crater, down the Tseax Valley and finally along the south bank of the Nass. It reaches a maximum width of about 10 km towards the downstream end. Available evidence, (1) and (5) among others, points to the year 1750 as a reasonable estimate of the date when the flow occurred. Whatever the year, Indian legends (14) consistently refer to spawning salmon in connection with the event, so evidently it occurred or continued into the fall.

A significant geological feature that played some part in bringing white settlers to the Kitsumkalum Valley, is a belt of gold-bearing quartz veins cutting through the Nass Range from northwest to southeast. It appears to be about 30 km wide and to extend from the Skeena River to Kitsumkalum Lake. In fact, the belt continues on the east side of the Skeena to the headwaters of Telkwa and Zymoetz Rivers. Unfortunately, as the 1930 Minister of Mines annual report explains, the "gold belt" lies within a region where the scouring effects of alpine glaciation were greatest. This accounts for the absence of the rich placer deposits that might otherwise be expected. Enough placer gold was found, however, to attract many of the early settlers.

Characteristic of the Nass Range are the numerous east-west passes, all close to 1200 m in elevation, that cut across the well defined north-south spine. Several small glaciers remain in north- and east-facing basins. Minor, low-elevation glaciers occupy the narrow, west-facing basins at the heads of Glacier and Goat Creeks. There are many small lakes within the range, the largest being Fiddler Lake in a deep, steep-sided basin at the head of Fiddler Creek.

Timberline is generally close to 1200 m. Below that, the slopes are covered with hemlock, spruce, balsam and some large areas of cedar. On the west side of the range, the slopes below 1200 m are steep, but the underbrush is not too thick. In some places, there is actually little or no underbrush, so access to timberline is feasible even without a trail. On the east side, it is a different story. Not only is it steep, but the devil's club seems to be particularly well developed, so taking a direct line through the thick, bush is almost out of the question.

The Nass Range is far enough inland to get much less rain and snow than typically coastal areas. Also, the weather tends to be more stable and predictable, but not to a degree that makes it safe to forget about it.

A large population of goats inhabits the area, but because their range is relatively accessible and to permit scientific studies of the goats, hunting has been closely controlled there for some time. Salmon runs in the adjacent Skeena and Kitsumkalum Rivers and good berry crops on the lower slopes of the Nass Range, makes it prime habitat for both black bears and grizzlies. The area is considered good moose country, but there are few deer. Enough fur-bearing animals inhabit the area to support some trapping.

HISTORICAL NOTES

The Skeena River, that forms the eastern boundary of the range, is one of the major rivers in the Province and historically very significant. In the days before railways and roads, the main rivers were the most important transportation routes for both people and freight. For hundreds and possibly thousands of years, the Skeena has served the Indians not only as an abundant source of fish, but as the prime route linking the coast and the interior plateau. From the early 1860's and for the next half century, white people also depended on the Skeena as their communications lifeline. That era ended in 1914 when trains started running on the Skeena line. Not surprisingly, the history of the Skeena and adjacent communities has been well documented (15). The community of Terrace dates back only to 1911, although by then several small communities had already been established nearby. The history of Terrace and surrounding areas has been recorded in a book (11) commissioned by the Terrace Public Library to mark the 1971 British Columbia Centennial Year. Since such historical accounts and others are readily available at local public libraries, the following notes deal mainly with historical events that are related directly or indirectly to trail development.

The first prospecting in the area was done by people travelling along the Skeena and their activities were confined to the immediate vicinity of the river. Placer gold was discovered in Lorne Creek as early as 1884 by Harry McDame, who eventually moved on to the Omineca gold fields via Hazelton and the Babine Trail. Various individuals kept working the placer deposits on a small scale for the next 15 years. Then, in 1899, the existence of an ancient, buried channel of Lorne Creek was recognized. This had escaped the effects of glacial scouring and was expected to yield worthwhile quantities of gold. Early attempts at hydraulic gravel excavation were discouraging, but in 1902 operations on a larger scale got underway and in 1914, operations intensified again. Considerable gold was recovered over the years, but in 1917 large scale operations came to an end.

At the same time as Lorne Creek was first worked for placer gold, so were adjacent Fiddler Creek and other creeks in the vicinity. Of these, only Douglas Creek yielded significant values of gold. Interestingly, Douglas and Lorne Creeks originate in almost the same place, but the former flows into Kitsumkalum Lake and the latter into the Skeena. As late as 1932 there was still considerable activity on Douglas Creek and a trail construction program was carried out there by the Department of Mines. The main trail up the true left bank of Douglas Creek came quite close to linking up with a trail cut from Ritchie, a flagstop on the CN Skeena line, to the head of the north fork of Lorne Creek.

The initial discovery of gold- and copper-bearing bearing quartz in the vicinity of Usk in 1894 led to a rush of claim staking in the surrounding area. By 1910, there were about 200 claims there on deposits containing gold, silver and copper. Once construction of the Grand Trunk Pacific Railway had started, and particularly after it was completed in 1914, prospecting and follow-up exploration got another boost. Most of the work was done close to the railway, but there were exceptions, such as the claims at the 900 m level on Knauss Mountain. Work there eventually led to construction of an access road from the railway line at Dorreen. That road had become so overgrown a few years ago that it was virtually impassable. Other old access routes to various claims, from points of departure up and down the railway, have also more or less vanished over the years. A trail still shown on some older maps, starts from what was Copper City Station, right across the Skeena from the mouth of Zymoetz River, and goes up Mt. Vanarsdol. Very little remains of that trail today. A 30 km trail starting at Ritchie, cut in 1930 to provide access to claims at the head of Lorne Creek, is now so faint in places that it is difficult to follow.

While settlements were springing up along the Skeena on the east side of the Nass Range, settlers were also moving up the Kitsumkalum Valley on the west side. At one time there were homesteads all the way up the valley to beyond Kitsumkalum Lake. The community of Rosswood flourished, complete with sub-post-office, at the north end of the lake. To make a living, the settlers had to turn to various activities other than just homesteading. Prospecting was one that, with luck, promised good returns. As a result, silver, lead and zinc discoveries were made north of Rosswood in about 1914. Later, about 1920, gold associated with lead and zinc was found at the Bear and Black Wolf claims on Maroon Mountain. Some gold was recovered from the former claim in 1923 using a small mill, parts of which can still be seen. At the Black Wolf claim, some high grade ore was produced between 1925 and 1928 and about 50 tons were packed out (16). As a legacy of this activity, an excellent trail, constructed with government assistance, still leads to the old claims on Maroon Mountain. Other trails were built up Wesach Creek north of Maroon Mountain and Maroon Creek to the south. Of the latter, constructed in 1921 with assistance from the Department of Mines, only the last few kilometers remain. The rest of it has been obliterated by logging. Even the remaining section has become inaccessible because the logging road leading to it is so eroded and overgrown as to be virtually impassable.

FUTURE PROSPECTS

The Nass Range has many attractive attributes from an outdoor recreation point of view. It is compact, scenic and close to the population centres of Terrace and Kitimat. Weather conditions are better than in other nearby areas and the access potential is very good from both sides of the range. Access from the east will almost certainly improve as a result of pressure from the logging industry. Incidentally, that may open up some interesting east-west traverse routes. One such route, from Ritchie to Rosswood via the old Lorne and Douglas Creek trails, could be opened up at any time with a relatively modest amount of effort. All that is needed is to locate, clear and mark the old trails. The result would be an interesting 50 km route, suitable for a three-day weekend trip. Moving south, the traverse routes would become shorter, the shortest being one from Usk to Terrace via Kitselas and Vanarsdol Mountains, an easy one day hike.

A more ambitious undertaking would be to establish a north-south ridge route extending from Maroon Mountain to Terrace. It would exceed 80 km in length and it should be possible to stay at or above 1200 m all the way. Convenient access from the south would be simply a matter of clearing and marking the old Mt. Vanarsdol Trail. At the north end, Maroon Mountain Trail already provides good access. The old mining road from Dorreen to the base of Mt. Knauss could be cleared for intermediate access from the east and on the west side of the range, the old logging road up Glacier Peak could be cleared to provide intermediate access.

Looking across Kitsumkalum Valley to Nass Range from Sleeping Beauty.

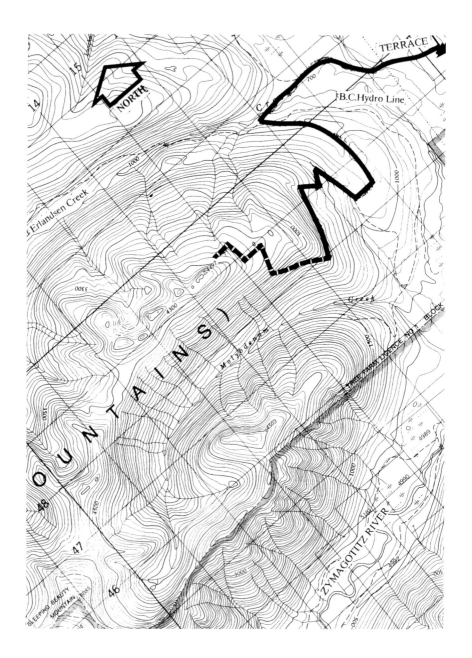

SLEEPING BEAUTY TRAIL [NR1]

(Part of Map 103I/10)

1cm=2/3km, 100ft.(30m) contour interval

SLEEPING BEAUTY TRAIL [NR1]

LOCATION:
West of Kitsumkalum River, near Terrace.

MAPS REQUIRED:
103I/10 Terrace (1:50,000)
103I Terrace (1:250,000)

ROUTE DESCRIPTION:
A good trail, 2 to 3 km from start at elevation 700 m to timberline at 1200 m. At first it climbs steeply to the top of the cut block, then the grade moderates as the trail winds its way up Erlandsen Ridge on a series of switchbacks. The made trail ends at a lovely little semi-alpine lake, but a trail of sorts continues up the ridge beyond. For some distance the going is quite good and it is well worth the effort to reach the first of many minor summits along the ridge. At an elevation of nearly 1400 m, it is well above timberline and the views, back towards Terrace, to the north up Kitsumkalum Valley and south out over the Skeena and beyond, are superb. To the west, on the far side of a low saddle and still a long way off along the ridge, is Sleeping Beauty Mountain. To reach it requires a lengthy and tiring sidehill traverse on the south side of the ridge.

Allow 1-2 hours up the trail to timberline and about 1 hour down.

DIRECTIONS:
Heading west from Terrace on Hwy.16, and just after crossing Kitsumkalum River, turn right (north) onto the Nass Road. About 9 km from the highway, take a side road to the left. There should be a signpost at the junction pointing the way to Sleeping Beauty Trail. At km 1, the road passes under a powerline. It continues in the same general direction for another 2 km and then heads more westerly until it crosses Erlandsen Creek at km 4. Right after the crossing, the road turns sharply left and heads southeasterly up the hill, only to bear gradually right again so that at the end of another 2 km it is heading southerly. There it makes a sharp right turn and, once across the ridge, half a kilometer or so farther on, another sharp right at a 4-way junction brings it onto a northerly heading. Keep on in that general direction for just under 1 km, then turn left and cross the creek. On the other side, the road bears left and, except through a switchback, continues steeply up across the slope in a southwesterly direction for close to 2 km. There it ends, some 9 km from the Nass Road junction and at an elevation of 700 m. The trail is well marked and heads up the slope where the road ends.

Except for the last 2 km, the access road should be passable for standard vehicles. That last section is steep and rough so it is more likely to be fit for 4-wheel drive vehicles only, if it is passable at all.

COMMENTS:

From Terrace, or when approaching by road from the east or south, look up, and there west of town, as if carved in stone on a grand scale, the profile of a sleeping woman stands out on the skyline. Sleeping Beauty Mountain is aptly named and a prominent Terrace landmark, typical of mountains that hikers want to climb!

As a local initiative, an access trail was constructed a few years ago from the end of the nearest logging road. It is now a designated Forest Service Recreation Trail, T6 on the Terrace-Nass Recreation Sites map. The trail is also described in another guidebook, "Hiking the Rainforest: Prince Rupert to Terrace", by Shannon Mark and Heather McLean (17).

When it is possible to drive right to the trail head, Sleeping Beauty Trail does provide quick, easy access to timberline and the kind of panoramic views one might expect from a mountain that is itself so visible. Otherwise the trail is not in any way remarkable and it only provides good access to a limited alpine area.

Children should find the trail short enough that they have no time to get bored before they are up in semi-alpine terrain. There they will find a delightful, miniature landscape of small trees, streams and ponds where the games that can be played are limited only by the imagination. At the right time of year, the blueberries are an added attraction.

Those intent on reaching the summit of Sleeping Beauty should bear in mind that it is a good 7 km distant, on the far side of a low saddle in the ridge and 600 m above the point where the trail leaves the timber: a very long day's hike there and back.

Sleeping Beauty and Mt. Kenney from end of trail.

46

MAROON MOUNTAIN TRAIL [NR2]

LOCATION:
Nass Range, near Terrace.

MAPS REQUIRED:
103I/15 Kitsumkalum Lake (1:50,000)
103I Terrace (1:250,000)

ROUTE DESCRIPTION:
An excellent trail, about 4 km from the start at elevation 500 m to timberline at 1350 m. Just below timberline, at about 1250 m, the trail forks. To the right, the trail climbs quickly onto the prominent west ridge immediately north of Hall Creek, where it ends. The left fork climbs slowly around the north side of the ridge. Above timberline it becomes quite faint in some places, but is reasonably easy to follow for another 3 km or so, past a couple of small lakes and then down to the remains of some old cabins.

From the end of the road, the trail starts out as a skid road angling steeply up the slope on a southeasterly heading. It intersects the trail proper near the top of the cut block at elevation 600 m, where the trail is heading gently up across the slope in a northeasterly direction.

This old pack trail winds its way up the steep slope, through open timber, in a series of well laid out switchbacks over the next couple of kilometers. It is a smooth, well defined trail with few, if any, windfalls. At about elevation 1000 m, the grade eases and the trail bears right to head more or less straight up the slope. It turns to the northeast again at elevation 1200 m and the left fork maintains that general heading right to the end.

Allow 2-3 hours from start of trail to timberline and just over 1 hour down from there.

DIRECTIONS:
From Hwy.16 on the west side of Terrace, turn north onto Kalum Lake Drive. It is a paved road that follows the east side of Kitsumkalum River and then Kitsumkalum Lake north to the small settlement of Rosswood. The lake comes into view 28 km or so from the highway and the next 6 km to the turn-off is a very scenic drive above the lake. Little more than 1 km after crossing Maroon Creek, take the side road angling up the hill to the right. A signpost identifies it as the access to Maroon Mountain Trail. Continue on up without any significant change in direction for 4 km to the ford across Hall Creek. The road is quite good and passable with a standard vehicle to that point. With 4-wheel drive, it may be possible to cross the ford and drive another 2 km, right to the start of the trail. Beyond Hall Creek, the road bears right and becomes a little steeper. About 1/2 km from the end, there is a sharp turn to right and the grade eases off. A signpost shows where the trail begins.

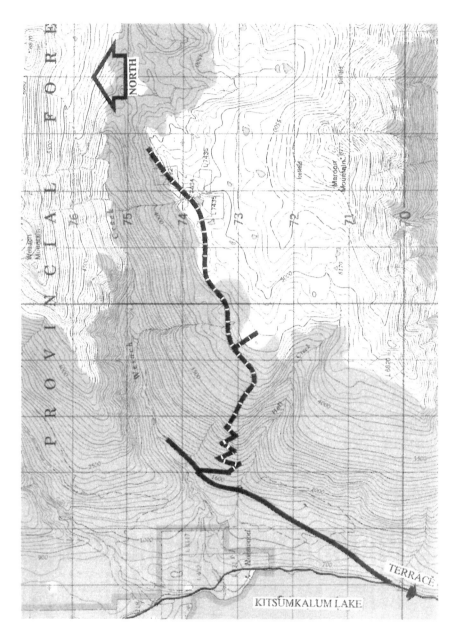

MAROON MOUNTAIN TRAIL [NR2]

(Part of Map 103I/15)

1cm=2/3km, 100ft.(30m) contour interval

COMMENTS:

This may be the best of the old pack trails in the whole area. It is very pleasant to walk on and provides quick, easy access to some fine alpine hiking country.

The trail was rebuilt with government assistance in 1929 and has been used and maintained fairly regularly ever since. Lately, the Forest Service has given it Recreation Trail status and it appears as Trail T1 on the Terrace-Nass Recreation Sites map. As a result, some work has been done in recent years on trail maintenance and more importantly on the access road, which was becoming overgrown to the point of being impassable. Modern logging roads are much inferior to the old pack trails in that they require far more frequent upkeep to remain passable.

Originally the trail started right from Kitsumkalum Lake near the mouth of Wesach Creek ,"just behind Olander's ranch", to qoute from the 1928 Minister of Mines annual report. It then more or less followed first Wesach and then Hall Creek up to the point where it is now joined.

As the trail approaches timberline, a lovely view opens up straight towards Wesach Mountain and a little farther on, the whole ridge becomes visible. The stark, reddish rocks make it an impressive sight, particularly when viewed against a clear, dark blue sky. The view is equally impressive back over Kitsumkalum Lake and the icefields and jagged peaks of the Coast Range beyond.

Maroon Mountain itself can be climbed quite easily from the north. It is a lovely peak with spectacular views in all directions and particularly towards the northeast of the majestic Seven Sisters.

This is great trail for children. It is short and easy enough that they do not get unduly tired or bored on the way up and once above timberline, the terrain is ideal for walking, running and playing. All the small lakes and streams add much to the enjoyment. Best of all perhaps, is that the trail allows children to run on the way down so they are likely to be way ahead rather than lagging behind and they are left with a favourable impression of the whole outing!

View towards Seven Sisters from Maroon Mountain.

49

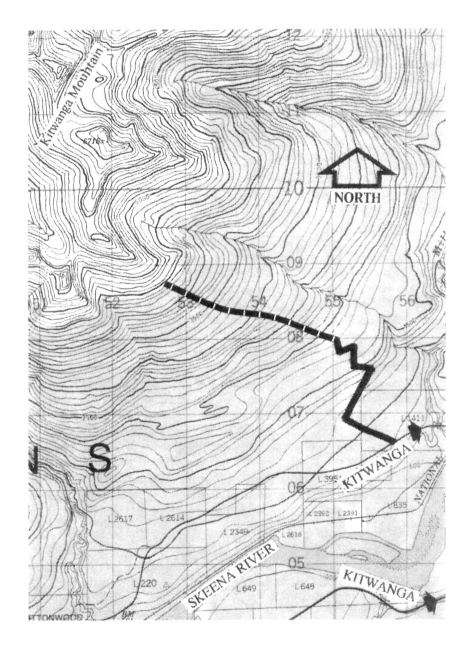

KITWANGA MOUNTAIN TRAIL [NR3]

(Part of Map 103P/1)

1cm=1/2km, 100ft.(30m) contour interval

KITWANGA MOUNTAIN TRAIL [NR3]

LOCATION:
Nass Range, near Kitwanga.

MAPS REQUIRED:
103P/1 Kitwanga (1:50,000)
103P Nass River (1:250,000)

ROUTE DESCRIPTION:
A steep, ill defined trail, about 2 km from start at elevation 550 m to timberline at 1350 m. It is essentially a direct line, on a bearing of approximately 270 degrees magnetic, from the end of a logging road, cut to intercept the lower end of an avalanche track. In distance, that is the half way point and the elevation is 900 m. To take advantage of easier going in the standing timber, the trail keeps to the southwest side of the slide path from there on.

Only here and there is there any relief from the uniformly steep grade. Fortunately the trees are spaced well apart most of the way up and there are not too many windfalls. The upper section, alongside the avalanche track, is the best part of the trail.

There are frequent blaze marks and the trail itself is becoming well enough worn that it is not really difficult to follow.

Those who can retain their motivation and keep going, should allow 2-3 hours on the trail to timberline. Getting down is very quick, 1 hour should be enough.

DIRECTIONS:
From Hwy.16, turn north onto Hwy.37 at Kitwanga and cross the bridge spanning the Skeena River. Turn left off Hwy.37 after 1 km and drive west along the back road to Cedarvale. In 1 km there is a bridge across the Kitwanga River and in another 2.5 km, the road crosses Mill Creek. Once across, it makes a sharp left turn before bearing right again to climb up a hill. Ignore the side road to the left at the base of the hill, but near the top, less than 1 km from Mill Creek, take the side road to the right. For the first kilometer, it traverses some fairly flat bench land, then it bears right and climbs quite steeply for the next kilometer after which it emerges into a logged area. Stay on the road that turns left up the hill with standing timber immediately to the right. Where that road bears left at the top of the cut block, take the older road that continues straight ahead and steeply up through standing timber. It soon bears right and shortly thereafter left and then left again to peter out about half a kilometer from the logged off area. At the last left turn, a skid road goes straight ahead up the slope. That is the start of the trail. The skid road also bears left very soon and then fades out. After a small, marshy pocket and some old stumps at that turning, look on the right

for a line of blaze marks to indicate where the trail heads up the slope. If it cannot be found after a quick search, the best move is to go straight up the fall line, using a compass to maintain a course of roughly 270 dgrees magnetic. Aim to avoid, to the left of the trail, some steep, rocky sections and to the right, a gully.

The initial, flat section of road is wet and full of deep holes, so only if it has been dry for some time, is it likely to be passable for standard vehicles. If so, it should also be possible to drive the next section to the logged off area. That is a gain of 2 km in distance and about 350 m in elevation. With 4-wheel drive, it should always be possible to get that far, but it would be unwise to count on driving any farther.

COMMENTS:

Getting to timberline on Kitwanga Mountain is a real grind because the trail is monotonously steep and there are no good viewpoints on the way up. However, on a nice day, anyone who perseveres is well rewarded. From no other vantage point is there such a breathtaking, superb view of the Seven Sisters. The magnificent north face of the massif is fully exposed in all its glory. Needless to say, camera and binoculars are essential items of equipment. It should be equally obvious that Kitwanga Mountain Trail is not suitable for most children, or for anyone else not prepared to invest considerable time and energy before being rewarded.

Kitwanga Mountain is itself quite impressive. What is visible from the highway is only the south end of an extensive ridge system that runs north for almost 20 km. The highest summit, at 2290 m, is 4 km back along the ridge.

Some may know or hear of this as the Bernadine Trail. It was apparently cut and blazed in the late 1970's by the Forest Service.

The Seven Sisters seen from Kitwanga Mountain.

TERRACE-SKEENA CROSSING AREA

The Skeena River forms the boundary to the west and north while the area is bounded in the south and east by the Zymoetz and Kitseguecla Rivers.

For close to 120 km, from Terrace to Skeena Crossing, Hwy.16 is confined to a narrow bench on the true left bank of the Skeena River by a rugged chain of prominent peaks, culminating in the Seven Sisters. The highest Sister, Weeskinisht Peak, soars to nearly 2800 m and surpasses all other peaks visible from the highway, not only in elevation, but in sheer visual impact. While it is an impressive chain of mountains from almost any vantage point, it is the north face of the range that is the most exciting prospect. Approaching from the north along Hwy.16, or even better, along the road or railway line on the opposite side of the Skeena, is an unforgettable experience. The Sisters rear up as a near vertical wall, from a base elevation of 200 m by the Skeena, to present in one graceful sweep almost the full vertical relief of 2500 m. In spite of the steep pitch, the north face is largely ice-encrusted. Crowning it all are the seven main peaks, jutting up in a line, like sharp, dazzlingly white fangs in the jaws of some immense beast. Even on the brightest day, the base of the wall is in deep shade, with the blue tones of the ice adding a mysterious and forbidding quality to the whole scene.

There are many other prominent peaks and some lovely alpine country in the Terrace-Skeena Crossing Area. Extensive prospecting and mineral exploration has been in progress there since the beginning of this century, mostly on the west side. Old trails exist on all the major creeks flowing into the Skeena and some are still passable. Consequently, access from Hwy.16 is fair to good. From the south, Kleanza Creek logging road provides some access, but it is virtually impossible to get into the area from the east.

GEOGRAPHICAL FEATURES

The mountains in the area can be viewed as continuous range, running in a north-south direction and forming the divide between the Skeena and Zymoetz Rivers. On the other hand, the range is so deeply cut by east-west valleys that, to some extent, it appears as a series of isolated east-west ridges.

Starting from the south, Treasure Mountain and the associated OK Ridge separate Zymoetz River and Kleanza Creek. Next, Bornite Mountain and connected ridges form the divide between Kleanza and Chimdemash Creeks. Between Chimdemash and Legate Creeks lies Mt. O'Brien with its ridges. Mt. Sir Robert separates Legate and Little Oliver Creeks and between the latter and (Big) Oliver Creek is Mt. Quinlan. At the north end, the lofty pinnacles of the Seven Sisters preside. Towards the south, peak elevations drop gradually to about 1800 m.

By and large, the rocks belong to what is known as the Kitselas Formation, consisting of volcanic rocks with some interbedded sedimentaries. They have been extensively intruded, and in some cases obliterated, by ig-

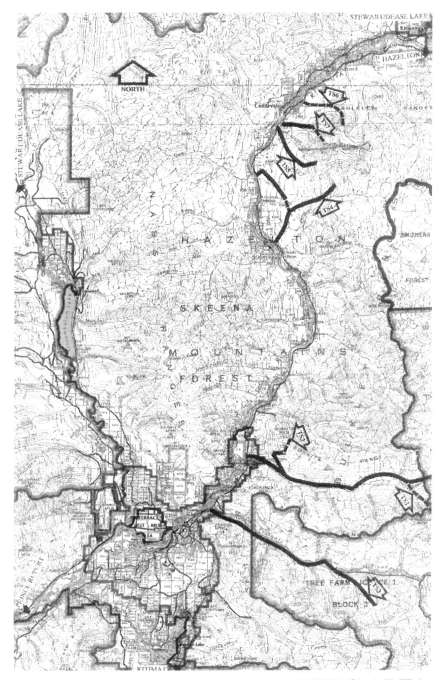

TERRACE-SKEENA CROSSING AREA

1cm=5km, 150m contour interval

54

neous dykes and stocks that are probably appended to the Coast Range batholith. The intrusions have caused more or less complete alterations, including mineralization, in the older formations. In fact, the area is noted for the number and variety of its mineral deposits. On the south bank of Zymoetz River, near the mouth of Kitnayakwa River, some interesting fossils occur right beside the road.

Although in retreat, the glaciers and snowfields along the spine of the range are still massive. As a rule, slopes are steep below the 1200 m level as a result of glacial grinding and rapid erosion by glacier-fed streams. Above 1500 m, the steep slopes are a consequence of late alpine glaciation. Between those elevations, the mountains are more smooth and rounded and exhibit fairly gentle slopes. This is thought to be the result of erosion, partly modified by continental glaciation (18). The particular topography has not favoured the formation of alpine lakes and there are few of them in the area.

Below timberline, which varies from 1200 to 1500 m, the remaining, unlogged slopes are well covered with hemlock, spruce, cedar, balsam and poplar. In the valley bottoms, the undergrowth tends to be very dense.

Steep slopes, deep canyons and dense underbrush make it unwise to attempt direct access routes to the mountains. It is even riskier to come off mountains on direct lines through unfamiliar terrain. The major creeks are typically too fast and cold to be forded without great difficulty. Even the trails along some of the bigger creeks have serious limitations as good access routes to the high country. Those that are still intact, typically gain elevation so slowly that a hike of 15 to 20 km is involved to reach the 500 m level.

While the area is quite far from the coast, the climate is almost coastal. The Skeena Valley acts as a conduit for moist, Pacific air which is then forced upwards by the mountains. Moisture condensing around the icy peaks, keeps them covered in cloud much of the time.

So much of the range is rugged and inaccessible that it supports a respectable population of mountain goats. On the other hand, for moose and deer, it is a somewhat hostile environment. Black bears are numerous and even the shy, roaming grizzlies find the area attractive. Not the least of the attractions are the salmon rivers that virtually surround the whole area. Small furbearing animals are quite common and some traplines are still being worked along the major creeks.

HISTORICAL NOTES

Much of the area's recorded history derives from prospecting and mining activity, although it was the Skeena River that attracted people in the first place. It was both a source of food and a vital transportation route for the Indians. White people used it as a route to the interior gold fields. On the way up the Skeena, the prospectors found placer gold on Kleanza and Chimdemash Creeks in the early 1880's. By 1892, sternwheelers were operating regularly on the Skeena.

The sternwheeler traffic brought into being the community of Kitselas at the downstream end of Kitselas Canyon. Hudson's Bay Company built a warehouse there in 1903 as a place to store merchandise and supplies waiting to get past the canyon. Later, as a result of speculation and some actual construction on the Kitimat-Omineca Railway, that was to link the interior with the coast via Telkwa Pass, Kitselas boomed. Even after Grand Trunk Pacific purchased the railway charter and decided to follow the west bank of the Skeena and to head for Prince Rupert rather than Kitimat, Kitselas continued to prosper as a supply depot and construction camp for the railway. However, once trains started running in 1914, Kitselas was left isolated on the wrong side of the Skeena. It went into a steady decline and eventually became a ghost town. Even the remains have gone. They vanished into the Skeena with a mudslide during the severe flooding of 1935 (11).

During the years when it appeared that the railway would be routed through Telkwa Pass, prospecting along the proposed route proceeded at a hectic pace. Maps included with the 1911 and 1914 Minister of Mines annual reports show numerous claims and an extensive network of trails radiating out from Kitselas. A main trail went up the Zymoetz River, starting on the south side, but crossing via a bridge to the north side after a few kilometers. The trail continued right through to the Bulkley Valley via Telkwa Pass after crossing the Zymoetz once again on a bridge opposite the mouth of Limonite Creek. A branch trail headed up Salmon Run River to claims on Treasure Mountain. Another branch went up the true right bank of Kitnayakwa River to coal claims on one of the tributary creeks. There was also a good trail all along the north side of Kleanza Creek, passing several claims on the way. It went on right past Kleanza Lake and dropped down again to the Zymoetz, where it joined the main Telkwa Pass trail. Branch trails, starting at the west end of Kleanza Lake, went to various claims on the north side of Treasure Mountain. At a later date, the Kleanza Creek trail provided access to claims at the head of Chimdemash Creek (Silver Basin) via a trail branching off near the confluence of the north and south forks of Kleanza Creek. Trails went up Bornite Mountain to access various claims there.

Many of the names given to creeks and mountains in the vicinity relate directly to mineral exploration. Treasure Mountain has been the scene of much prospecting and mining activity, mainly concerned with copper, silver, lead, zinc and gold deposits, from the beginning of this century to the present. In the 1911 Minister of Mines annual report, Kleanza Creek is referred to as Gold Creek. Interestingly, the creek that originates in the same pass, but flows east into the Zymoetz, is called Nogold Creek! Bornite Mountain was so named when hunters and trappers, in about 1890, found pieces of bornite float in creek beds and slides at higher elevations.

After Kitselas ceased to be the major centre, prospecting activity spread north to the other large creeks flowing into the Skeena. In the 1920's, the basins where Chimdemash, St. Croix and Legate Creeks have their origins, came in for a lot of attention. As this activity intensified, a direct route was developed up Chimdemash Creek. For the first few kilometers it followed the south bank and then switched to the north bank of the creek. A branch trail was constructed up the north fork to claims above timberline, while the main trail continued on to Silver Basin at the head of the south fork. St. Croix and Legate Creeks both had trails leading to claims near their headwaters. Legate Creek trail was reached by a ferry service across the Skeena from Pacific, at the time a divisional point on the CN line.

Most of the trails were either built or improved with substantial grants from the Department of Mines. The quality of the trails and the intensity of exploration can best be judged by considering that in 1929, a 37 kW generator, driven by a Pelton turbine, was transported about 8 km up the Chimdemash Creek trail and installed at the junction of the north and south forks. There the equipment was installed to serve exploration work high up on the north fork via a transmission line. The major equipment was later removed, but the old powerhouse is still visible as are the penstock and tailrace conduits. It is also possible to see where the trail and powerline headed up the steep gully of the north fork. Unfortunately, the trail has been vitually obliterated by undergrowth, slides and erosion. The same is true for St. Croix Creek trail. On Legate Creek, as late as 1969, a 20 km road was pushed in along the creek to reactivate several old claims in the basin behind Mt. O'Brien. Copper, lead and zinc showings were fairly promising. That road was so poorly routed and constructed that it has almost completely gone. A logging road now penetrates about 15 km up the valley, but the bridges at the many creek crossings either have been, or are soon likely to be, washed out, so the upper reaches of Legate Creek are again virtually inaccessible.

Claims on the Seven Sisters are first mentioned in the 1925 Minister of Mines annual report. They were located just below the 1500 m level, about 12 km from the present highway, and were reached by a trail from Cedarvale. By 1929, several groups of claims were being actively explored. In the late 1960's and early 1970's, the area was again under scrutiny and access roads were pushed in along the old trail to the Seven Sisters group and the trail to the Waverley group, at the 1200 m level north of (Big) Oliver Creek.

The history of Cedarvale dates back to 1887 when it was founded as a Christian village by Rev. Robert Thomlinson (15). Miniskinish was the name chosen for the village and it is so identified on a map in the 1911 Minister of Mines annual report.

Except for a few scattered and mostly shortlived settlements, such as Kitselas, Copper City, Usk and Miniskinish, the east bank of the Skeena between Terrace and Skeena Crossing remained isolated and sparsely inhabited to as late as 1944, when Hwy.16 finally connected Prince Rupert, Terrace and Hazelton. It was not much like a highway in those days. In fact, it was a narrow, twisting dirt track, in places hugging the shores of the Skeena and in others, high above the river. Even as late as the 1960's, not much had changed. However, in the years since, it has been gradually improved to the point that the description "highway" now fits reasonably well.

It was in the roadless era prior to World War II that the first recorded mountaineering took place in the Seven Sisters area. N.M. Carter of Prince Rupert was much impressed with what he saw when he had his first view of the range from across the Skeena, on board the train. In 1939, he organized the first of many expeditions to climb Weeskinisht Peak, which he knew to be over 2700 m. The approach was by train to Cedarvale and then by ferry across the Skeena with packhorses, supplies and equipment. As a result of unfavourable weather conditions, it was only on his third attempt, in August 1941, that the summit was reached (13). None of the other Sisters were climbed until 1962 and the last one was first climbed in 1968 (2).

In an area with so little recorded climbing history, it was a remarkable coincidence that at the time of Carter's first attempt on Weeskinisht in 1939, there was in fact another party of climbers in the field, all set to climb the same peak! When H.S. Hall and H. Fuhrer became aware of Carter's expedition and his longstanding interest in the Seven Sisters, they graciously decided to climb some other mountain. The one they chose was an un-named peak, south of and somewhat higher than Mt. Sir Robert. They were successful and recorded an altitude of nearly 2500 m at the summit.

FUTURE PROSPECTS

With some exceptions, the mountains and alpine country in this area have more to offer mountaineers than casual hikers and skiers. Access routes tend to be long and the terrain above the valley bottoms is precipitous. The few remaining trails and other access routes are mostly in poor condition.

It seems likely that an area so well and variously mineralized will continue to attract mineral exploration. However, unless some particularly rich ore body is uncovered, such activity will probably involve only helicopter traffic and cause relatively little conflict with recreational activities.

The most serious conflicts will continue to be generated by logging activity. The Kleanza and Legate valleys have been virtually stripped of timber and if logging is to continue as exemplified by the ravages inflicted there, the outlook is not bright. A battle is still raging about logging around the Seven Sisters. The Seven Sisters Wilderness Society has fought long and hard to have the area set aside as a park. If that fails, there is still hope that the Society's efforts will lead to logging practices that are ecologically and aesthetically more acceptable than might otherwise have been the case.

Although logging has to a large extent supported the local economy in the past, it cannot continue for long at the present rate of cutting. Hopefully by choice, but if not by hard necessity, when the economically recoverable timber has been exhausted, other foundations for the economy will be developed. So long as areas like the Seven Sisters remain unimpaired, a lively tourist industry, based on people who come to look, photograph, climb, ski, hike and therefore remain in the area for some time, can be one such foundation. Some investment will be required to restore and construct trails. Many interesting routes could be developed, e.g. right around the Seven Sisters and possibly an exciting ridge route all the way from there south to Kleanza Lake.

TREASURE MOUNTAIN TRAIL [TS1]

LOCATION:
Terrace-Skeena Crossing area, near Terrace.

MAPS REQUIRED:
103I/8 Chist Creek (1:50,000)
103I/9 Usk (1:50,000)
103I Terrace (1:250,000)

ROUTE DESCRIPTION:
Just short of km 27 on Kleanza Creek logging road (sign-posted as Bornite Mountain Road at turn-off from Hwy.16), go due south, straight down the bank, from the road to the west end of Kleanza Lake which is only a very short distance away. Cross the creek immediately downstream of the lake. The trail, such as it is, continues straight ahead, quite close to the lakehore. At the other side of the lake, the trail climbs diagonally up the short, steep hill from left to right and then crosses an open, marshy area. The heading remains almost due south towards South Kleanza Creek. It is not worth looking for signs of the trail across the open area, but beyond it, the sketchy trail follows the true right bank of the creek up.

A good 2 km from the lake, starting at about elevation 1100 m, semi-open scree slopes show up on the other (south) side of the creek. Rather than trying to follow what little is left of the trail, it is better to cross the creek and simply pick the easiest route up to the 1400 m saddle straight ahead. From the saddle, the 1900 m summit of Treasure Mountain, 2 km away, can be reached without any great problems.

From the road to the saddle it is only just over 4 km and the gain in elevation 700 m. Allow 2-3 hours up and 1-2 hours down.

DIRECTIONS:
About 15 km east of Terrace on Hwy.16 is the signposted turn-off to Kleanza Creek Provincial Park campsite. Instead of continuing along Kleanza Park Road to the campsite, immediately turn left onto Bornite Mountain Road which goes up the hill and then bears right. After 4.5 km, there is a signposted turn-off on the left to Bornite Mountain Trail [TS2]. Just beyond, on the main logging road, is a gate that could be locked. Check ahead of time with Repap in Terrace to find out. If it is going to be open long enough to get in and out, it is clear sailing all the way to km 27 on a good road.

COMMENTS:
This trail is all that remains of an extensive trail network that linked the Kleanza, Zymoetz and Chimdemash valleys in the early years of this century. The Kleanza trail started from the community of Kitselas at the junction

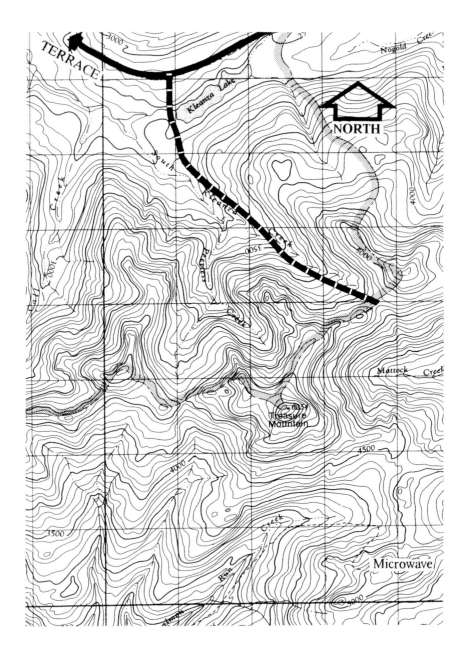

TREASURE MOUNTAIN TRAIL [TS1]

(Part of Map 103I/9)

1cm=1/2km, 100ft.(30m) contour interval

of Kleanza Creek with the Skeena. It followed the creek up past a number of claims, including placer gold claims about 8 km upstream. The main trail followed the north shore of Kleanza Lake, then it cut across to Nogold (previously Flat) Creek and followed it part of the way down to the Zymoetz River. It eventually reached the Zymoetz just downstream of the junction with Mattock (then Bell) Creek. Near the mouth of Limonite Creek (then known as Summit Creek) was a bridge across the Zymoetz and there the Kleanza trail met a trail coming up the true right bank of Zymoetz River. That was a major trail connecting the lower Skeena with the Bulkley Valley via Telkwa Pass. It also gave access to iron ore claims on Limonite Creek.

On the east side of the Zymoetz, a side trail crossed a bridge to the south side of Limonite Creek and continued south to Kitnayakwa River, a tributary to the Zymoetz. After following the Kitnayakwa up for a short distance, the trail turned east up Gabriel Creek to some coal claims.

Near where Treasure Mountain Trail branched off to follow South Kleanza Creek up, another branch headed up Call Creek and across to Peerless Creek, the location of other claims. In fact, the whole of Treasure Mountain was well covered by claims and could also be reached from the south by a trail branching off from the main Zymoetz River trail. There is now a road, more or less where the trail was, starting up from the mouth of Salmon Run Creek, that provides access to a B.C.Tel microwave repeater on the south ridge of Treasure Mountain. Unfortunately, that route requires the use of a private cable car to get across the Zymoetz. Nobody should make the mistake of going down that way after coming up from Kleanza Creek, since fording the Zymoetz is beyond the capabilities of the average hiker.

The original access to the upper reaches of Chimdemash Creek, an area referred to in old mining reports as Silver Basin, was via a branch of the Kleanza trail that went up along the tributary immediately downstream of North Kleanza Creek. Only later was a trail constructed up Chimdemash Creek from the Skeena.

Although Treasure Mountain Trail is now in poor condition, it is short and even if it cannot be found, the going fairly easy. Treasure Mountain is a worthwhile destination because of its strategic position in the big bend of the Zymoetz. Consequently, it commands outstanding views, to the east, through Telkwa Pass and to the southeast and south of the spectacular Howson Range and the major peaks immediately west of Clore River. Signs of mineral exploration abound. Most of the activity took place prior to 1914, while Telkwa Pass was still being seriously considered as a route for the northern rail link to the coast, but there has been some recent activity also.

It is worth noting that the main logging road continues a long way past km 27 and Kleanza Lake. It crosses the divide and starts to follow Nogold Creek down, but whereas the old trail turned right, the road bears left to eventually follow Zymoetz River upstream. The view east across the river is very impressive, as might be expected, since the chain of peaks there is really an extension of the mighty Howson Range to the north of Telkwa Pass.

Treasure Mountain; trail leads to saddle on the left.

Looking NW along the ridge at the head of Chimdemash Creek.

BORNITE MOUNTAIN TRAIL [TS2]

LOCATION:
Terrace-Skeena Crossing area, near Terrace.

MAPS REQUIRED:
103I/9 Usk (1:50,000)
103I Terrace (1:250,000)

ROUTE DESCRIPTION:
This is an old packtrail, well laid out and maintained. Most of it has been superseded by logging roads and only about 2 km remain from the end of the road at elevation 900 m to timberline at 1400 m.

The general heading is easterly as far as the remains of some old cabins at the 1200 m level, then the trail turns more northerly for the last kilometer. It eventually leads to old mineral claims just over the divide between Kleanza and Chimdemash creeks.

To reach the 1780 m summit of Bornite Mountain, follow the trail up to the crest of the ridge. The summit is then in clear view to the northwest, so it is simply a question turning left off the trail and picking the easiest route along the ridge.

Allow 1-2 hours from start of trail to the ridge and 1 hour or less down.

DIRECTIONS:
Proceed from Terrace as for Treasure Mountain Trail [TS1], but at the Bornite Mountain Trail sign, 4.5 km from Hwy.16, turn onto the side road that angles up the hill to the left. From the turn-off to the trail head it is close to 8 km and the gain in elevation is about 600 m. For the first kilometer or so, the road heads southeasterly and then it makes a sharp turn to a northwesterly heading. It maintains that general heading for 3 or 4 km as it climbs steadily and then for the last 3 km, it switchbacks up, ending on an easterly heading. There are signposts at some of the corners where it is not obvious which is the right road and at the end where the trail starts up the slope.

With 4-wheel drive, the road should be passable all the way, but with a standard vehicle, only count on being able to drive about half way up.

COMMENTS:
Particularly when it is possible to drive right to the end of the road, this trail offers easy access to Bornite Mountain and the ridge that extends east from there for 20 km to the head of Chimdemash Creek. The only obvious destination is the summit of Bornite, but hiking along the ridge in the opposite direction is pleasant enough. Both ways there are many lovely little lakes and the view is great in all directions. Some vantage points offer an impressive view down the steep slopes into Chimdemash valley.

The twin peaks of Bornite Mountain from end of trail.

Bornite Mountain Trail is well suited for children because it is short and easy. Once above timberline, the ridge is an exciting playground where they can keep occupied for hours. Older children who have done some hiking can easily reach the summit and still have time and energy left to roam around at the top, enjoy the view and maybe wander over to the other summit. Since the trail is so good, children may well insist on running all the way down.

When snow and weather conditions are favourable, Bornite Mountain is worth considering as a place to go skiing. It is a great run down the road and above timberline on the ridge, the possibilities are endless. The trail is short enough that even if it is not ideal for skiing, it is not a serious obstacle.

The Forest Service lists this as Recreation Trail T2 on the Terrace-Nass Recreation Sites map and undertakes a certain amount of road and trail maintenance from time to time.

BORNITE MOUNTAIN TRAIL [TS2]

(Part of Map 103I/9)

1cm=1/2km, 100ft.(30m) contour interval

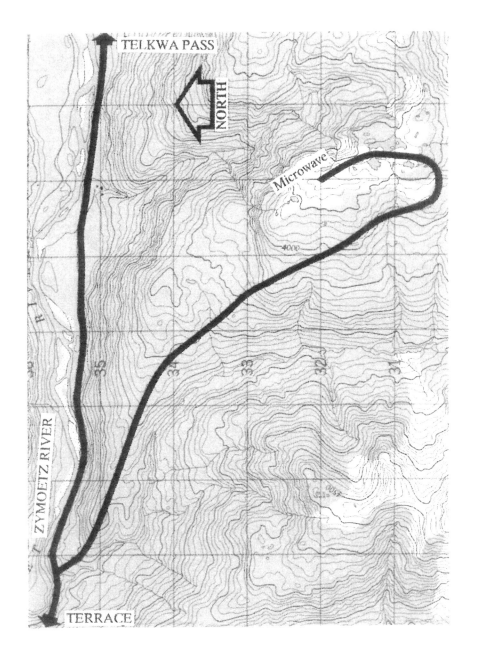

TRAPLINE MOUNTAIN ROAD [TS3]

(Part of Map 103I/8)

1cm=1/2km, 100ft.(30m) contour interval

TRAPLINE MOUNTAIN ROAD [TS3]

LOCATION:
Terrace-Skeena Crossing area, near Terrace.

MAPS REQUIRED:
103I/8 Chist Creek (1:50,000)
103I/9 Usk (1:50,000)
103I Terrace (1:250,000)

DIRECTIONS:
Just before Hwy.16 crosses Zymoetz River about 6 km east of Terrace, turn right to access km 7 of a parallel logging road immediately south of the highway. Turn left onto the logging road and follow it up the true left (south) side of the Zymoetz to km 29. On the right is a building and then a side road with a gate that may be locked. The road climbs, over a distance of 10 km, on an easy grade, from elevation 200 m at Zymoetz River to the 1450 m summit of Trapline Mountain. The logging road is generally good and quite suitable for standard vehicles. Trapline Mountain Road may also be passable for standard vehicles all or part way if the gate is not locked.

COMMENTS:
The road is maintained by B.C.Hydro to service a microwave repeater station on Trapline Mountain. Looking northeast, the line-of-sight to the next station, at the head of Winfield Creek [TR7], is through Telkwa Pass. To the west, the nearest repeater is on Copper Mountain [KT5].

Trapline Mountain is a somewhat isolated, rounded hump projecting just above timberline, which is at about 1400 m. The alpine area is fairly extensive and harbours many small lakes. As might be expected, such a location offers some excellent views in almost every direction. In particular, the Howson Range to the east is an impressive sight. When it is possible to drive up, Trapline Mountain is a great place to take visitors who want to see and photograph the magnificent Coast Range mountains without expending much time or energy. Equally, it is good place to take young children and introduce them to the many lovely and unique features of alpine environments.

Trapline Mountain Road is not a very exciting hike, nor does it lead to anywhere of great interest, but when snow conditions are good, it is well worth skiing up for the sake of the long, gentle run down. In the summer, just substitute a mountain bike for the skis to enjoy the descent.

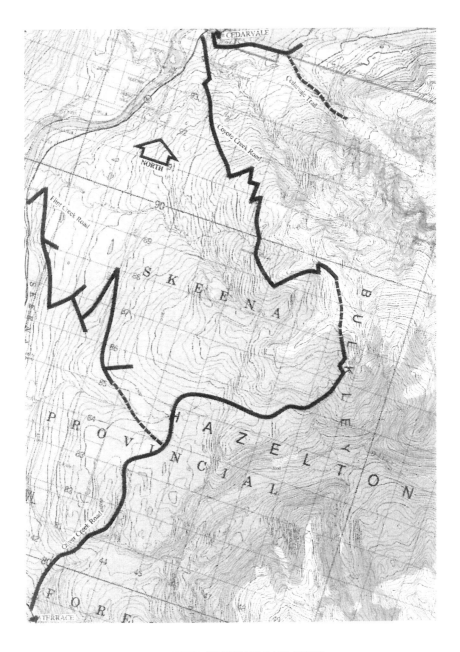

OLIVER CREEK ROAD [TS4]
COYOTE CREEK ROAD [TS5]
CEDARVALE TRAIL [TS7]
(Part of Maps 103I/16 & 103P/1)
1cm=1km, 100ft.(30m) contour interval

OLIVER CREEK ROAD [TS4]

LOCATION:
Terrace-Skeena Crossing area, near Cedarvale.

MAPS REQUIRED:
103I/16 Dorreen (1:50,000)
103I Terrace (1:250,000)

DIRECTIONS:
Some 50 km east of Terrace, and 22 km west of Cedarvale, along Hwy.16, an old mining access road climbs steeply up the hill on the east side of the highway. At the turn-off, there is big stockpile of gravel used for highway maintenance and lots of room to get off the road and park. A signpost indicating the start of Oliver Creek Road may be in place.

The elevation at the highway is about 150 m. From there, the road climbs steeply for 5 km or so to an elevation of 750 m where it flattens out and skirts the west side of a small lake. For the next 3-4 km, there is very little gain in elevation and much of the road is a series of mud holes.

Just over a kilometer from the first lake is a second one with a small trapper's cabin. Shortly thereafter, a "cat" track joins the road from the left. It is the connecting link to Flint Creek logging road, that in turn joins Hwy.16 about 11 km east of Oliver Creek Road.

When the road starts going up again, it climbs quite steeply for 3 km to 1100 m, but after that, for the next 3 km or so, there is little change in elevation as it contours around the south flank of the Seven Sisters. For the last kilometer or so, the road is heading north up a draw, straight towards the Seven Sisters. It is a stiff climb, from near timberline at 1200 m to 1450 m where the road ends.

Even with 4-wheel drive, Oliver Creek Road must be, for all practical purposes, classed as impassable. On the other hand, Flint Creek logging road is good enough for standard vehicles. As long as that is the case, it is an easier and quicker route. The "cat" track across to Oliver Creek Road starts at an elevation just over 700 m some 10 km from Hwy.16. Flint Creek logging road leaves the highway a short distance west of Flint Creek, about half way between Cedarvale and Oliver Creek Road. When the twists and turns are discounted, the effective heading is southeasterly, which takes the road to within a couple of kilometers of Oliver Creek Road.

COMMENTS:
Flint Creek logging road offers some attractive views of the Seven Sisters and back, across the Skeena, of the Nass Range. Other than that, there is not much to be seen until the 1100 m level is reached. Mt. Quinlan then comes into view to the southeast, on the other side of Oliver Creek. As the

Along Oliver Creek Road; the curtain rises on the Seven Sisters.

road heads up the final draw, the Seven Sisters are not visible, but from the ridges on either side, they are an impressive sight. The view is magnificent beyond words and almost has the impact of a shock wave as the ridge east of the road is breasted. There, straight ahead, looms the massive south face, surmounted by a serrated line of peaks, sharply etched against the sky and buttressed by a great icefield that fills the foreground. Looking back down the road and across Oliver Creek, lovely Mt. Quinlan is the inevitable centre of attention.

By continuing northwesterly, up the draw beyond the end of the road, it is easy to cross over a ridge and contour around the head of an intervening basin, at about the 1700 m level, to link up with the top of Coyote Creek Road [TS5]. The road is clearly visible from the ridge as it cuts across the sidehill on the far side of the basin.

Oliver Creek and Flint Creek roads are both well suited for skiing in the winter as is some of the area above timberline that they lead to. However, the Seven Sisters have some rough, steep terrain and are liable to attract all the bad weather that comes along, so they must be approached with care and the right knowledge and equipment.

While Flint Creek logging road is generally a better starting point than Oliver Creek Road, the advantage dwindles when a mountain bike is used. If it has been dry for some time, the relatively level sections of Oliver Creek Road may not be so muddy as to interfere with cycling. Then the time it takes to get up and down that road should not be much more than when starting and finishing at the top end of Flint Creek road.

COYOTE CREEK ROAD [TS5]
(Route map on p.68)

LOCATION:
Terrace-Skeena Crossing area, near Cedarvale.

MAPS REQUIRED:
103I/16 Dorreen (1:50,000)
103I Terrace (1:250,000)

DIRECTIONS:
Almost 70 km east of Terrace and 3 km before reaching Cedarvale, Hwy.16 crosses Coyote Creek. Less than a kilometer from the bridge on the Terrace side, Coyote Creek Road branches off from the east side of the highway. At first it is actually a section of old, paved highway, but then it heads east, past a dump site, to the base of a hill where it turns right and starts to climb steeply. For the next 9 km, the general heading is southeasterly and the road continues to climb steeply, almost without interruption, from an elevation of 150 m at the highway to timberline on the crest of a ridge at 1400 m. A kilometer or so before the crest is reached, there is a side road to the left that leads to an old mining camp. Beyond the crest, the road continues for a couple of kilometers, heading northeasterly as it climbs the sidehill on the far side of the ridge. Towards the head of a large basin, close to elevation 1600 m, it fades out in the scree slope among the rocks.

COMMENTS:
The road is not only steep but rough. Some sections have been deeply eroded by run-off and some are badly overgrown by alder. Even with 4-wheel drive it is impassable. There are no views to speak of until near timberline. The major attraction is that Coyote Creek Road offers the quickest and most direct access to the Seven Sisters. On reaching timberline, the rewards more than compensate for the effort and tedium of getting there.

The chain of peaks that constitutes the Seven Sisters is without equal in the whole of West Central British Columbia. On all counts, it can only be described by superlatives. It is more beautiful, more impressive, more inspiring and in a sense more aloof than any of the other mountains and ranges. Those with some mountain hiking experience will understand the distinction between being in the mountains and being on a mountain. The Seven Sisters do not invite that distinction, mere humans are always on them and never completely at ease.

There is not a great deal of level ground for camping. The ridges are sharp, the slopes steep and the exposures spectacular. Even from the end of the road at 1600 m, most of the range is fairly inaccessible. Weeskinisht Peak is still higher by nearly 1200 m and not safely within reach of anyone lacking mountaineering experience and equipment. Weather is always an element of uncertainty. Moisture anywhere in the region seems to find its way to the Seven Sisters to condense around the towering, ice-capped peaks and in the process, produce quite ferocious winds. In fine weather, a hike up some of the more accessible ridges, offering splendid views in all directions, is an unforgettable experience, but never forget to approach the Seven Sisters with all the respect and deference due to a reigning monarch.

From the end of the road, it is not difficult to link up with the end of Oliver Creek Road [TS4]. Simply contour around the head of the basin and cross over the ridge. The road should then be visible lower down on the far (east) side of the next basin.

**Borden Glacier, Mt. Sir Robert and Mt. Quinlan
from divide between Coyote and Oliver Creek Roads.**

WHISKY CREEK TRAIL [TS6]

LOCATION:
Terrace-Skeena Crossing area, near Cedarvale.

MAPS REQUIRED:
103I/16 Dorreen (1:50,000)
103P/1 Kitwanga (1:50,000)
103I Terrace (1:250,000)
103P Nass River (1:250,000)

ROUTE DESCRIPTION:
Start by scrambling up the steep sidehill on the north or true right bank of Gull Creek to reach an old, overgrown road, now barely visible from below. After making an initial switchback, the grade eases and the road heads easterly, up what becomes a fairly well defined draw. It stays on the true right of the draw and is easy to follow, but less than a kilometer from the highway, it switches to the other side. The crossing is not very obvious, but once across, the road is again well defined as it climbs up and over a minor ridge. Then it makes a pronounced curve to the right before bearing left again to resume its easterly heading. Soon after that, the road ends almost imperceptibly and the trail begins. Except for an area of windfalls, this part of the trail has been fairly well maintained and the going is good.

Some 2 km from the highway, the trail drops down slightly to cross Whisky Creek at elevation 400 m. On the far side, the trail bears more southerly and for a while follows the true right bank of the creek upstream. Then it gradually deviates from the creek and eventually starts to climb steeply up the ridge that lies northeast of Whisky Creek.

Beyond the crossing of Whisky Creek, there has been little if any effort to maintain the trail and some sections are very faint and hard to follow. Higher up on the ridge, where the grade eases again and the trail starts to contour around the head of a draw on semi-open sidehills, it becomes impractical to keep trying to maintain contact with the trail. The best course of action is to try picking the easiest route, on a southerly heading, to intersect Whisky Creek, while at the same time yielding as little elevation as possible. That should result in a return to the creek close to elevation 700 m and nearly 6 km from the highway. With luck, the trail, which essentially does the same thing, may be picked up again at some point. It makes little difference whether it is or not since the wide, open creek-bed upstream is the best route for the next kilometer or so. After that, keep to the open sidehill on the true right side of Whisky Creek to eventually reach the toe of the large icefield below the north face of the Seven Sisters.

Allow 3-4 hours up to timberline at elevation 900 m and only slightly less for the return trip.

DIRECTIONS:

After passing a cafe by the side of the road at Cedarvale, Hwy.16 heads east up a short hill, flattens out and then drops down towards the Skeena River again. Just as it starts down and about 2 km from Cedarvale, there is a signpost where the highway crosses Gull Creek. Look for the old side road at the top of the cutbank immediately after crossing the creek. The best place to park is a little farther along, on the side of the road nearest the Skeena.

COMMENTS:

The trail was cut originally in the late 1950's to access a molybdenum prospect near the head of Whisky Creek. It is not a good trail and the views are few and far between. Casual hikers are likely to find it long and tedious with little to reward them at the end. However, it should be of considerable interest to mountaineers who wish to come to grips with the forbidding, ice coated wall that is the north face of the Seven Sisters. Others may simply want to get onto the extensive icefield at its base and see the great north face at close range.

Whisky Creek Trail leads to foot of glacier on the right.

WHISKY CREEK TRAIL [TS6]

(Part of Map 103P/1)

1cm=1/2km, 100ft.(30m) contour interval

CEDARVALE TRAIL [TS7]

(Route map on p.68)

LOCATION:
Terrace-Skeena Crossing area, near Cedarvale.

MAPS REQUIRED:
103I/16 Dorreen (1:50,000)
103P/1 Kitwanga (1:50,000)
103I Terrace (1:250,000)
103P Nass River (1:250,000)

ROUTE DESCRIPTION:
A well maintained trail, starting at elevation 400 m and climbing, over a distance of about 3 km, to 750 m where it leaves the timber and ends among the jumbled rocks left behind by a retreating glacier. The snout of the glacier is visible higher up in the gully, but it is still a couple of kilometers away. To get there involves either scrambling up over a succession of open but rough terminal moraines or trying to pick the best route through the bush that has already become firmly established on the lateral moraines.

From the road, the trail heads straight up a dry ridge through open timber, it then bears right, crossing the ridge and dropping down slightly to cross the north fork of Coyote Creek after about one kilometer and at elevation 500 m. The trail then remains on the south side of the creek where it climbs quite steeply on a series of overgrown moraines. Shortly before it leaves the timber, the trail passes a small lake at elevation 700 m.

Allow about 2 hours up to the open moraine and a good hour down.

DIRECTIONS:
Proceed as for Coyote Creek Road [TS5], but turn east off the highway on the other (Cedarvale) side of Coyote Creek. Next, take the first turning on the left and almost immediately start climbing, heading initially towards Coyote Creek. The road then curves around to the left onto an easterly heading. About 3 km from the highway, at the top of the first large clear-cut, there is an area to turn around and park beside a small stream. The blaze marks and flagging of the well defined Cedarvale Trail should be visible directly above the parking area, at the edge of the standing timber.

Most vehicles should make it easily up the road to the start of the trail.

COMMENTS:
Cedarvale Trail makes it possible to get up and out of the timber quite quickly, without great effort, but the gully it leads to is a box canyon and virtually a dead end. Mountaineering skills and equipment are required to get out of it. However, the moraines, the glacier and the cliffs on either side are interesting and spectacular enough to make it a worthwhile destination.

Cedarvale Trail heads up the valley to the glacier.

For mountaineers, it is a short, direct access route to the whole, impressive north face of the Seven Sisters range. At the top of the headwall, the glacier merges with the icefield at the foot of the north face. Heading down and due north from there leads into the gully where Whisky Creek Trail [TS6] ends, making it a viable alternative exit route.

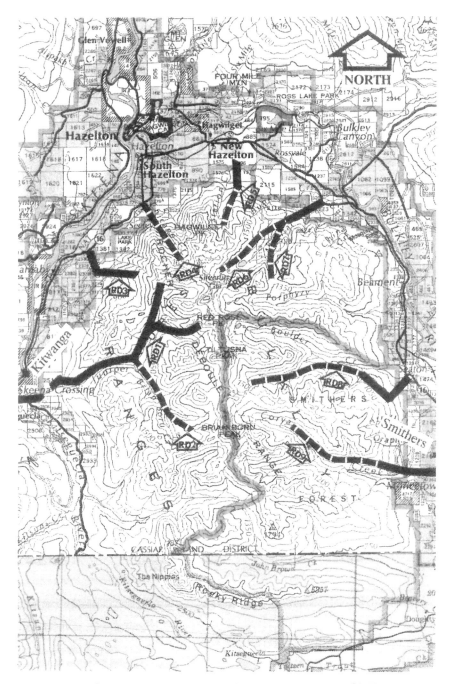

ROCHER DEBOULE RANGE

1cm=2.5km, 150m contour interval

ROCHER DEBOULE RANGE

This magnificent range, crowned by the 2500 m peak of Brian Boru, has a vertical relief of over 2000 m and extends 30 km along its major north-south axis. At its widest, it covers nearly 25 km from east to west. It is outstanding in every sense of the word. As an isolated massif, bounded by the deep, wide valleys of the Bulkley, Skeena and Kitseguecla Rivers, it stands out physically and dominates the skyline on approach from either east or west along Highway 16.

The prominent northern extremity of the range, Hagwilget Peak, soars above the valley floor at Hazelton, presenting an almost sheer, 1500 m north face that commands attention and fires the imagination. At the south end of the range, a major east-west ridge, that terminates in the west with the Nipples, is hardly less spectacular, not so much from the highway, but certainly from adjacent ranges.

Not the least outstanding feature is the excellent access from all directions afforded by Highway 16 and the railway that follow the Bulkley and Skeena Rivers around the east, north and west sides of the range, and by side roads from Skeena Crossing and near Moricetown on the south side. Generally good trails located on most of the principal creeks and rough roads up Juniper and Comeau Creeks, provide easy access to the interior of the range.

GEOGRAPHICAL FEATURES

The thick series of sedimentary and volcanic rocks that form the bulk of the range are invaded by numerous granodiorite stocks related to the batholithic rocks of the Coast Range mountains some 50 km to the west. Those granitic intrusions are of special interest since they and the invaded rocks near them contain all the significant mineral deposits.

The range is dominated by a major north-south spine of high pyramidal peaks and connecting knife-ridges. Numerous lateral ridges extend east and west from the central spine. Variations in type and hardness of the rock have greatly influenced erosion patterns and hence the present appearance and characteristics of the range. Glaciation has been another contributing factor. It appears that the high peaks projected above the Cordilleran ice sheet even at its greatest extent. A number of small alpine glaciers still remain on the east side of the central spine, but they are all receding. Below 1700 m, the ridges and passes have been rounded by ice movement. Several small lakes have formed behind terminal moraines left by the retreating glaciers.

Timberline is generally around 1400 m. The slopes below are well covered with hemlock, spruce, cedar, balsam, jackpine and poplar. Although the undergrowth is light on some of the north-facing slopes, it is not generally safe to assume that it is easy going where there are no roads or trails.

Because of the relatively small area, easy access and intense exploration and mining over an extended period, Rocher Deboule Range is no longer prime habitat for mountain goat and grizzly bear, however, both species can still be seen. Other large mammals such as moose, deer and black bear are probably as plentiful as ever. Wolverines, wolves and smaller furbearing animals can be seen occasionally, but as they are very shy, sightings are rare. Above timberline it is unusual not to see or at least hear marmots.

Birds are plentiful, with all species present that are normally found at the latitudes and climatic zones represented.

MINING

Metals produced from the ores mined in Rocher Deboule Range include gold, silver, copper, tungsten and arsenic. Other metals such as uranium, cobalt and molybdenum are present in interesting amounts. The principal producing mines have been Rocher Deboule (copper) and Red Rose (tungsten). The known mineral showings are concentrated around the northern dome of porphyritic granodiorite.

Initial exploratory geological surveys were started around the turn of the century. Prospecting was sporadic prior to 1910, but then became more intense and most major properties were quickly discovered. Development lagged until completion of the railway in 1914 and the advent of high copper prices during the latter part of World War I. Prices fell sharply again in 1919 and put a stop to most activity. A rise in metal prices in 1929 did not last, but when Asiatic sources of tungsten dried up in 1941/42 as a result of World War II, it became profitable to produce tungsten from Red Rose Mine. That came to an end with the War. The last period of prosperity came in 1950/54 with the first widespread search for uranium. At the same time copper went up in price and with the Korean War, tungsten was again in short supply, so Red Rose Mine was back in operation until it finally closed in December 1954.

Apart from Rocher Deboule and Red Rose, the only property that ever amounted to anything was the Victoria Group of claims overlooking Seeley Lake. The initial discovery occurred in 1909. A carload of hand-sorted ore was shipped out in 1918 followed by a few odd carloads in later years.

Geological features and mining activities in Rocher Deboule Range are well documented in the series of annual reports of the B.C. Minister of Mines and summarized in two special publications (19,20). A legacy of all the mining related activity is a number of mostly well built trails leading to the interior of the range. While there are other legacies that might best be forgotten, the trails are a priceless heritage that must be cared for to serve a population that will find them increasingly important to access the beauty and challenges of Rocher Deboule Range.

HISTORICAL NOTES

The particular location of Rocher Deboule Range and the conditions favouring mineralization have both had an important influence on the activities and settlements in adjacent valleys. By British Columbia standards, the area is rich in history and cultural features.

The confluence of the Bulkley and Skeena Rivers has been the site of native settlements going back into history (15). Hagwilget, one of the settlements, has retained its separate identity, the other, Gitenmaks, is now part of Old Hazelton. The site invites settlement. Among other advantages, there is a large area of flat bottom-land, exceptionally good fishing and two major natural trading routes between the coast and interior pass through there. Hazelton was the point where goods had to be transferred from canoe or riverboat to man or horse for overland transport along the Babine Trail. The other route was by water up the Nass and then overland by the Grease Trails to Hazelton.

So firmly were historical trading patterns established that the initial attempt by Hudson's Bay Company to set up a trading post there in 1866 was not successful. The post was closed down in 1868 and Hudson's Bay Company did not return to Hazelton until 1880 when the Skeena had become firmly established as a choice route to the interior for white trappers and prospectors (15). The importance of Hazelton as a traditional site of native settlements has been recognized by the establishment there of 'Ksan, a reconstructed Gitksan Indian village and museum.

An overland telegraph line linking Europe and North America via Alaska and Siberia was laid out to pass through Hazelton. In 1866 work parties arrived to clear the right-of-way. The scheme was dropped the same year when an underwater cable across the Atlantic at long last became operational. By then the line had reached Fort Stager at the junction of the Skeena and Kispiox Rivers and the right-of-way had been partly cleared to a point 300 km north of Hazelton on Telegraph Creek. Many of the people who found themselves out of work stayed on in the area as prospectors. It was these people and others that followed who, without capital or equipment, had the determination and fortitude to invest incredible amounts of time and labour in construction of the trails they needed to reach and work their claims.

Interest in the telegraph line revived in 1898 on account of the Klondike Gold Rush and in 1901 it was completed. The line remained in operation long after the Gold Rush had come to an end, until 1936 in fact, as a communications link with Alaska. That year record level floods wiped out large sections of the line and trail bringing to an end a colourful chapter of northern history.

Initially as a result of favourable reports from Hudson's Bay Company people about the promising agricultural prospects in the Bulkley Valley and subsequently, promotion by the government and speculators, settlers began to arrive early in this century. The influx was spurred on by the prevailing spirit of adventure and by generally depressed economic conditions. These early settlers came via either the Cariboo wagon road and Blackwater trail or by riverboat up the Skeena to Hazelton.

The area's potential was considerably enhanced by talk of a possible railway to the coast. It eventually materialized in 1914 and set the stage for more rapid development. A shorter rail route through Telkwa Pass was seriously considered, but rejected in order to serve existing settlements along the Bulkley and Skeena Rivers.

FUTURE PROSPECTS

With its many attractions for hikers, climbers, photographers and amateur geologists, as well as easy access from all directions, it is somewhat surprising that Rocher Deboule Range is not more heavily utilized by area residents and tourists oriented to outdoor recreation. The trend will certainly be towards more use being made of the recreational resources of the range. Just how quickly that happens depends to some extent on how urgently the people of the Hazeltons feel the need to broaden the local economic base.

World metal prices could rise again to levels that make mining profitable. There is the potential therefore for conflicts between mineral and recreational resource users. To such conflicts there are no general solutions. Each conflict will require a particular solution that can only be sought intelligently by people who know what resources exist and their actual and potential value in the local scheme of things. Hopefully the high potential value of the recreational resources of Rocher Deboule Range will be recognized.

Tiltusha Peak and Brian Boru from Red Rose mine.

JUNIPER CREEK ROAD [RD1]

LOCATION:
Rocher Deboule Range, near Hazelton.

MAPS REQUIRED:
93M/4 Skeena Crossing (1:50,000)
93M Hazelton (1:250,000)

DIRECTIONS:
At Skeena Crossing, about 19 km east of Kitwanga and 25 km west of New Hazelton on Hwy.16, turn onto a logging road, signposted Kitseguecla Road, that branches off easterly, away from the Skeena. Follow it for just over one kilometer, then turn left onto Juniper Creek Road. At the fork immediately thereafter, keep to the right. For the first 6 or 7 km, the road remains almost level and in places comes very close to Juniper Creek. Then it climbs quite steeply away from the creek before the grade eases again. There is a fork 11 km along Juniper Creek Road. Turn left for the site of the old Rocher Deboule mine and right for the old Red Rose mine site. The distance from the fork to either one is about 3 km, and both are located near timberline at elevation 1200 m.

COMMENTS:
If the road is passable, it provides easy access right to the interior of Rocher Deboule Range, however, the condition of the road is quite unpredictable. Where it runs close to Juniper Creek, it is subject to washouts and in other places it may slide out or be covered by mud slides. At times it has been so overgrown as to be virtually impassable. Fortunately, from time to time, the outlook for mineral exploration has been favourable enough to warrant restoration of the road, after which it has remained passable for some years. In the summer of 1988 it was in such good condition that standard vehicles could drive up. Generally it is best to assume that 4-wheel drive and lots of clearance will be required to drive much beyond the first 6 km. To reach the Red Rose mine site involves fording Juniper Creek about a kilometer beyond the fork. Until late July or early August, that may present a problem.

So long as the road remains in reasonable condition, a mountain bike is a good alternative to a 4-wheel drive vehicle as a means of access. Skiing up the road in the winter also makes access quite easy, however, the steep slopes and narrow valleys, so characteristic of Rocher Deboule Range, means difficult ski terrain and great potential for avalanches. Except for expert backcountry skiers, it is just not worth the effort to ski up the road.

While the debris surrounding the mine sites, left behind by extensive mining and exploration over a long period of time, is undoubtedly an eyesore,

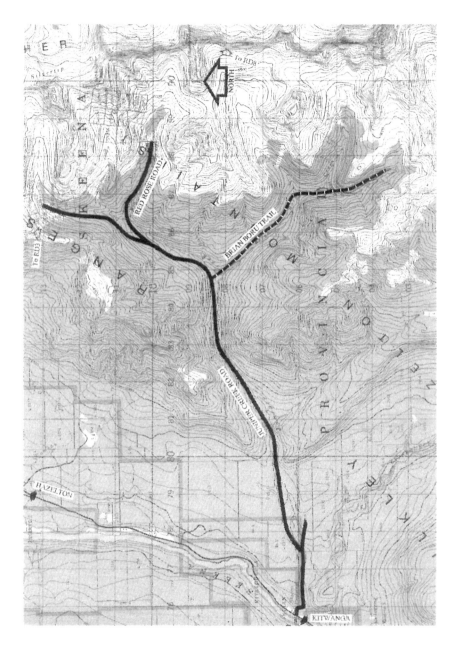

JUNIPER CREEK ROAD [RD1]
BRIAN BORU TRAIL [RD2]
(Part of Map 93M/4)

1cm=1km, 100ft.(30m) contour interval

it does make the area interesting and exciting, particularly for children. Considerable supervision is required since the various old structures are mostly in an advanced state of decay.

Most of the mine workings and prospects are high up on the mountain sides, consequently there are many old roads and trails that continue on up. Above Rocher Deboule mine, at the head of Juniper Creek, the terrain is somewhat less precipitous than around Red Rose, where there are fewer routes up and hiking is more difficult.

For anyone with no particular objective in mind, a hike to the top of the ridge west of Rocher Deboule mine is well worth the effort. There are fine views in all directions, to the west and south out over the Skeena Valley and north and east towards the main ridges and valleys of the range. Particularly impressive is the view east into Armagosa basin, where the rock is quite red, and beyond, where the upper workings of Red Rose mine can be seen. At the low point on the ridge are the remains of the top structure of an aerial tramway. This was used to convey ore down to the railway line along the Skeena during the initial operation of the mine. From the top of the tramway, an old overgrown trail heads down northwesterly and eventually intersects Comeau Creek Road [RD3], but it is now easier to go up the ridge for half a kilometer or so and then follow a lateral ridge down. It is not a problem to find a route down the north side of that ridge into the basin where Comeau Creek Road ends.

Via the main ridge system it is possible to link up with Chicago Creek Trail [RD4], Station Creek Trail [RD5] and Blue Lake Trail [RD6], but such traverses should only be attempted by experienced and properly equipped climbers and mountain hikers.

The Red Rose branch of the road provides access to within 3 km of Tiltusha Peak, which at 2400 m is the second highest of the range. Via a pass just south of the peak, it is possible to cross over to the top of Boulder Creek Road [RD8]. Another possibility is to continue south and around the basin at the head of the north fork of Brian Boru Creek. Beyond is a saddle and another basin. Over the next ridge is the top end of Brian Boru Trail [RD2].

Rocher Deboule mine and Red Rose mine both have long and fairly interesting histories. The former was originally staked in 1910 and considerable copper ore bodies were blocked out during the next few years. In 1914 a narrow-gauge railway, about 3 km long, was built from a portal at elevation 1550 m to carry ore to an aerial tramway that took it down to a siding, known as Tramville, on the new railway by the Skeena. Remains of the narrow-gauge railway, the top tramway structure and some of the intermediate towers can still be seen.

Operations continued off and on until late 1918 and again during 1929 and 1930. In 1950 the property was acquired by Western Uranium Cobalt and work started on a grand scale. New mine buildings, bunkhouses and a school were built. A 1600 horsepower hydroelectric plant was constructed on Juniper Creek. Some of the penstock concrete supports and remains of the dam can still be seen from the road, about 7 km from the highway. Upstream, the transmission line right-of-way and a few power poles are still visible. A 100 tons per day mill went into operation in the summer of 1952. It was shut down shortly thereafter and part of it was moved to Red Rose mine, then owned by the same company. There it operated until that mine too was shut down in 1954.

Although all the veins of Rocher Deboule mine are mildly radioactive, copper was the principal ore mined, most of it in 1915 and 1916. Gold, silver, lead and zinc were significant byproducts.

Red Rose was discovered in 1912. During the next seven years, the property was thoroughly prospected with the interest centering on gold, silver and copper showings. Little attention was paid to a large quartz vein in which tungsten bearing minerals were found in 1923. However, when Asiatic sources of tungsten were cut off during World War II, a mill was put in to process the Red Rose ore. The mill operated through 1942 and 1943. After that the property remained inactive until 1951 when Western Uranium Cobalt took it over and operated it until 1954.

View towards Seven Sisters from divide between
Juniper and Comeau Creek Roads.

BRIAN BORU TRAIL [RD2]
(Route map on p.84)

LOCATION:
Rocher Deboule Range, near Hazelton.

MAPS REQUIRED:
93M/4 Skeena Crossing (1:50,000)
93M Hazelton (1:250,000)

ROUTE DESCRIPTION:
From the confluence of Brian Boru and Juniper Creeks at elevation 700 m to the remains of an old prospector's cabin at 1200 m on the south fork of Brian Boru Creek, it is just over 6 km. The trail is not in very good condition. Parts of it are somewhat overgrown and there are many windfalls across it. Some work has been done to maintain the trail in recent years, but more needs to be done. It is not overly difficult to follow as far as the cabin site, but after that, pick the easiest route up the ridge in a southeasterly direction to reach open country.

The trail follows the east side of Brian Boru Creek quite closely most of the way, but opposite the mouth of the north fork it switches to the west side for a short distance before returning to the east side of the south fork. To find the start of the trail is a little tricky. The problem is that the original location of Juniper Creek Road [RD1] was closer to the creek and then it switchbacked up to the level where it is now. Part of that old section of road has been washed out just where the trail used to start. To reach the junction of Brian Boru and Juniper Creeks and get onto the trail now, it is best to stay on Juniper Creek Road for about 8 km to elevation 750 m, which is shortly after the grade eases at the end of a steep climb away from the creek. Keep looking across the creek to the southeast and when Brian Boru valley appears to be directly opposite, head down through bush on a bearing of 140 degrees magnetic to intersect Juniper Creek about half a kilometer from the road. The mouth of Brian Boru Creek, on the other side of Juniper Creek, should be in sight or at least not far away. Getting across to the start of the trail, just upstream of the junction, requires fording Juniper Creek, unless there is a log in place there.

Allow a good 4 hours from the start of the trail to open country and not much less for the return trip.

DIRECTIONS:
Proceed as for Juniper Creek Road [RD1], follow it for about 8 km and search for the start of the trail as explained above. There is no obvious place to turn around and park at that point, but it is not really difficult.

COMMENTS:

Given the state of the trail, it of limited interest except as an access route to Brian Boru Peak, which at 2500 m is the highest in the range. Other possibilities are to cross the spine of the range to link up with either Boulder Creek Road [RD8] or Corya Creek Trail [RD9]. By remaining just west of the spine and following it to the north, it is pleasant hike, well above timberline all the way, from the end of Brian Boru Trail to the Red Rose mine site [RD1].

The Brian Boru group of claims was located in 1914 or 1915, but little work has been done there since the late 1920's. The claims are situated at the 1600 to 1700 m level on the southwest slope of the west ridge of Brian Boru Peak. On some editions of the 93M/4 map sheet, they are shown incorrectly on the north fork of Brian Boru Creek. That at least is consistent with the similarly incorrect location of the trail on some editions of map sheet 93M!

Brian Boru from end of trail on west ridge.

COMEAU CREEK ROAD [RD3]

LOCATION:
Rocher Deboule Range, near Hazelton.

MAPS REQUIRED:
93M/4 Skeena Crossing (1:50,000)
93M Hazelton (1:250,000)

DIRECTIONS:
About 12 km southwest of New Hazelton, shortly after passing Seeley Lake Provincial Park, turn left (south) off Highway 16 on to Comeau Road. It is a good gravel road about 2 km in length. Just before it ends, there is a house with a red roof on the right and a rough gravel road, which is Comeau Creek Road, on the left (east). From the turn-off at elevation 300 m, Comeau Creek Road climbs quite steeply over the next 6 km to timberline at elevation 1250 m. The road essentially follows a subsidiary ridge in an easterly direction all the way. It is well constructed and except for a few wet areas in the beginning, the surface is firm and dry. Under average or better conditions, it should be possible to drive a standard vehicle about half way up and thus gain 400 m or so in elevation. Under best conditions or with 4-wheel drive, the road is passable very nearly to the end. It is not difficult to find places to turn around.

COMMENTS:
Beyond the end of the road, on the other side of the draw, a trail continues on for the best part of a kilometer to an elevation of nearly 1800 m. This was the site of the Victoria mine. Some old structures and parts of an overhead tramway are still visible. The associated cabins were located where the road crosses the draw, but they have all been obliterated.

By going on up the draw and then climbing out of it to the right (south), it is easy to follow the ridge up to where it intersects the main ridge overlooking Juniper Creek. That ridge leads down into a saddle where the top structure of an old tramway is located. It was used at one time to convey ore from Rocher Deboule mine down to the railway line at Tramville, near what is now Carnaby. The top structure is visible from the highway and also when driving up Comeau Creek Road. From a few places, it is even possible to see the remains of some of the intermediate structures.

An overgrown trail leads from the top tramway structure back down to the top end of Comeau Creek Road. It is not too difficult to follow, except near the end where it meets the road. On the other hand, it is not serious to loose the trail there. Simply head due north across the easiest ground to eventually intersect the road. On the other side of the ridge, there is a connecting trail from the tramway structure down to Juniper Creek Road [RD1].

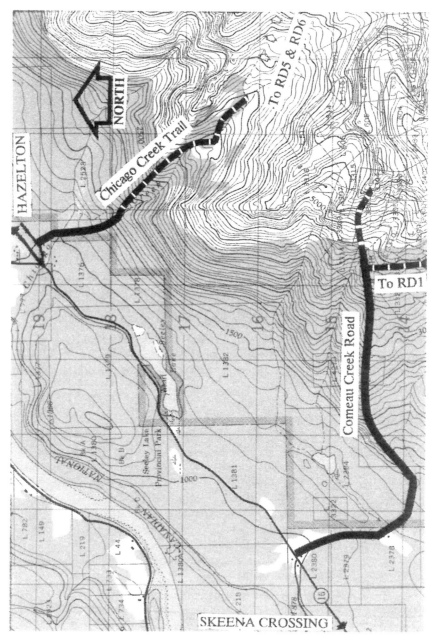

COMEAU CREEK ROAD [RD3]
CHICAGO CREEK TRAIL [RD4]
(Part of Map 93M/4)

1cm=1/2km, 100ft.(30m) contour interval

Above Victoria mine at the end of the main trail, there is a system of sharp, serrated ridges that can only be traversed safely by very experienced and well equipped mountain hikers and climbers. Via those ridges, it is possible to link up with Juniper Creek Road [RD1], Chicago Creek Trail [RD4], Station Creek Trail [RD5] and Blue Lake Trail [RD6].

Comeau Creek and Juniper Creek Roads provide easy access to the major mining areas of Rocher Deboule Range and should be of particular interest to people with some knowledge of geology. Children will find it an exciting area since there is a profusion and great variety of relics from the mining era as well as "pretty rocks" to be seen.

The top of the road and beyond is a great place for photographers with a spectacular, almost birds-eye view of the highway and river immediately below and impessive views to the north of Hazelton and the Skeena and Kispiox Valleys.

Comeau Creek Road ends in gully below peak.

CHICAGO CREEK TRAIL [RD4]
(Route map on p.90)

LOCATION:
Rocher Deboule Range, near Hazelton.

MAPS REQUIRED:
93M/4 Skeena Crossing (1:50,000)
93M Hazelton (1:250,000)

ROUTE DESCRIPTION:
Approximately 3 km from start of trail at elevation 350 m to open country at 1100 m where the trail fades out. A fair trail, reasonably easy to follow most of the way. It keeps to a well defined ridge on the true right (east) bank of Chicago Creek for half its distance, climbing steeply through fairly open timber. Higher up, it traverses a progressively steeper sidehill through heavier timber. Although the trail grade becomes less steep, the undergrowth gets worse and the trail overgrown in places.

Just beyond the half way point, at about elevation 900 m, the creek becomes accessible for a short distance. Most of the way it is not since the trail is either high above it or the creek flows underground. Near the end, the trail crosses the creek and for a short distance stays on the west side before returning to the east side. At that point, it becomes too indistinct to be followed easily, but the timber is patchy at that elevation, so a trail is not needed.

Allow 3-4 hours up to open country and 2 hours down.

DIRECTIONS:
Follow Highway 16 southwest from New Hazelton for 7 km. Turn left (south) on to Richmond Frontage Road. A road to the right goes to South Hazelton. Richmond Frontage Road immediately turns sharp left to parallel the highway and is a good place to park. Right away, two roads go off to the right. The second one provides direct access to Chicago Creek Trail. Unfortunately, it crosses a small area of private property and goes very close to a house, so it is necessary to ask for permission to use it. It continues on as a "cat" road, immediately crosses Chicago Creek and then goes up the true left bank of the creek for about 1 km to a water system intake. Go back across the creek at the intake and straight up the steep bank to the top of the ridge where the trail runs.

COMMENTS:
Chicago Creek flows down a steep, narrow gully that is filled with boulders higher up. Much of the creek flows under the boulders, so is out of reach. There are few tributaries and the result is that drinking water is not accessible much of the way.

Although the timber is not heavy, there is no view to speak of except occasionally back along the trail. By moving to the west side of the valley, it is possible to get out into open country quite low down, but the boulders make it rough going, so it is best to keep to the trail. Very little water and flat ground make it virtually impossible to camp anywhere along the trail.

The ridges enclosing the bowl at the head of the creek are spectacular. There are interesting routes for experienced mountain hikers and climbers across and along the ridges to link up with Station Creek Trail [RD5] and Blue Lake Trail [RD6] to the east and with Juniper Creek Road [RD1] and Comeau Creek Road [RD3] to the west.

Due to the condition of the trail, the scarcity of good views and the long, steep climb up, this trail is not generally recommended, except as an access or exit route for experienced and very fit hikers and climbers.

**Chicago Creek Trail heads up the steep valley
on the right; on the far left is Hagwilget Peak.**

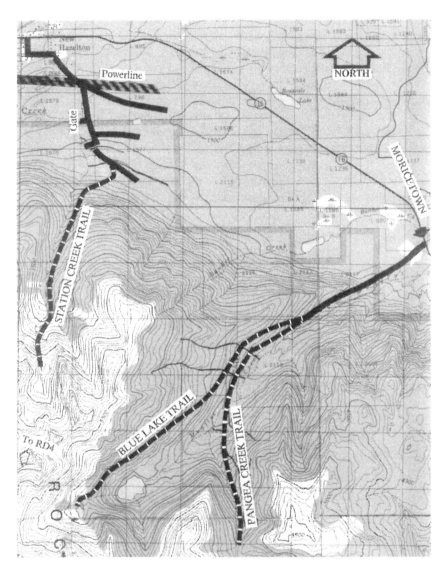

STATION CREEK TRAIL [RD5]
BLUE LAKE TRAIL [RD6]
PANGEA CREEK TRAIL [RD7]
(Part of Maps 93M/3&4)

1cm=2/3km, 100ft.(30m) contour interval

STATION CREEK TRAIL [RD5]

LOCATION:
Rocher Deboule Range, near Hazelton.

MAPS REQUIRED:
93M/4 Skeena Crossing (1:50,000)
93M Hazelton (1:250,000)

ROUTE DESCRIPTION:
Approximately 3 km from start of trail at elevation 500 m to semi-open country, elevation 1250 m, where trail becomes indistinct. A well defined, good trail that stays on the true right of Station Creek and climbs very steeply on switchbacks through heavy timber most of the way. Over the last kilometer or so, the grade gradually eases off as the trail works its way into a small bowl. At the back of the bowl, the trail bears right for a short distance before it heads up a steep, boulder-filled gully where it peters out. The gully leads up into a larger, alpine bowl at elevation 1550 m.

At the beginning, the trail is mostly level or climbing gently. On the left, a logged off area is just visible through the standing timber. The noise from Station Creek may be barely audible on the right, but it gradually becomes louder as trail and creek converge. The creek then remains within earshot all the way up.

Allow 3-4 hours to get up into the top bowl and a good 2 hours down.

DIRECTIONS:
Turn south off Highway 16 onto McLeod Street in New Hazelton. At either 12th or 13th Avenue, turn left and shortly thereafter turn right (south) onto McBride Street. After a 1/2 km, the continuation of McBride, which is actually the old road to Telkwa, crosses under a powerline. Continue on for another 1/2 km or so to where a side road goes right to New Hazelton's water reservoir. It has a gate with a "no entry" sign. With a standard vehicle, it is a good place to turn around and park. After following the main road for another 1/4 km, a side road goes left to a logged off area. Take the road to the right which ends a short distance beyond the fork. With 4-wheel drive, the road is passable to that point. An old road continues more or less straight ahead across a small stream. Either ford the stream or detour across dry ground to the right to get to it. The old road splits after a 1/4 km, but the two branches rejoin a little farther along, just before a small stream cuts across the road. Shortly thereafter and not much more than 1 km from the gated reservoir road, watch for Station Creek Trail going off to the right.

COMMENTS:
There are no views to speak of until the top end of the trail and then

only back down the valley to the north. Once in the first small bowl, the surrounding ridges come into view and are quite spectacular.

The main attraction of this trail is that it provides fast, uncomplicated access to the north end of Rocher Deboule Range. From the upper bowl, it is easy to reach the ridge system that eventually terminates in Hagwilget Peak. It is also fairly straightforward to link up with Chicago Creek Trail [RD4] and Blue Lake Trail [RD6].

Because it is so persistently steep and has few interesting features or views at lower elevations, the trail is not generally recommended except for hikers and climbers in good condition who intend to continue right up to the high ridges or peaks. However, anyone who wants to see a classic example of a well constructed packtrail and speculate on the cost of building its like today, should also find it interesting.

Those who do use the trail should make a point of taking a good look at the surrounding tangled mess of windfalls and try to imagine the horrors of getting through it without a trail. That is the quickest way to get some understanding of the immense value of such trails and the importance of preserving them.

Looking up Mudflat Creek; Blue Lake trail goes up the valley,
Station Creek Trail leads up to the far end of the ridge on the right.

BLUE LAKE TRAIL [RD6]
(Route map on p.94)

LOCATION:
Rocher Deboule Range, near Hazelton.

MAPS REQUIRED:
93M/3 Moricetown (1:50,000)
93M/4 Skeena Crossing (1:50,000)
93M Hazelton (1:250,000)

ROUTE DESCRIPTION:
About 6 km from start of trail at elevation 650 m to second lake where it ends at 1300 m. A good trail, well constructed and maintained, climbing gradually until it levels out high above Blue Lake. Over the last kilometer up to the second lake, there is only a 100 m gain in elevation.

For the first 1.5 km, the trail is actually sections of old logging roads crossing a clear-cut and climbing steadily to an elevation of 900 m at the edge of the standing timber on the far side. There is a signpost at the start and in a couple of other locations across the clear-cut, but a degree of vigilance is required to stay on the trail where the alder is encroaching. Bear in mind that there are no significant changes in direction and that if the trail is lost, it is only necessary to keep going straight ahead across the clear-cut and search for it again along the edge of the standing timber, about half way up the cut-block. The trail, once in the standing timber, crosses a small creek almost right away.

The next 3 km is a steady climb through open timber, very quiet and peaceful, but without any views. After that the view starts to open up and soon the trail cuts across the steep sidehill some 200 m vertically above Blue Lake.

Allow 3-4 hours up to the second lake and about 2 hours down.

DIRECTIONS:
Approximately 9 km east of New Hazelton on Highway 16, and just before Mudflat Creek crosses under the highway in a culvert, turn right onto a gravel road. Almost immediately the road forks. Keep to the right there, but at the next fork by a gravel pit, take the somewhat overgrown left fork. There may be a signpost indicating the Blue Lake route. Very shortly, a sketchy road forks left; ignore it and keep right. The road is passable for standard vehicles with good clearance over the next 2-3 km and with 4-wheel drive, it may be passable well up into the clear-cut. At the start of the clear-cut, a sign, marked Blue Lake Trail, shows where the road turns right up the hill.

**Ridge across Blue Lake
can be reached from
Pangea Creek Trail.**

COMMENTS:

Across the clear-cut and then through the timber, the trail is pleasant but unspectacular, without any views to speak of. Beyond that, the upper part of the trail is highly spectacular and particularly so where it skirts around high above Blue Lake. The colour of the lake is more commonly deep, emerald green than blue, but whatever its colour, it is a beautiful sight. There is an impressive waterfall where Mudflat Creek emerges from the second lake and plunges a couple of hundred meters into Blue Lake. Difficulties with both perspective and lighting make photography a real challenge.

The trail was previously known as Mudflat Creek Trail after the creek it follows up. However, some years ago the Forest Service sponsored a much needed trail restoration project, including signposting with the name Blue Lake Trail. "Blue Lake" was one of the two claims that the trail was originally built to serve; the other was "Black Prince". Certainly the new name is more in keeping with the real attractions of this lovely trail and should entice more people to explore it.

There are some good places to camp between the lakes with ample supplies of firewood and water. At the second lake there is not much flat ground, but no problems with water or firewood.

This is a good trail for family hiking once the children are old enough to enjoy the breathtaking scenery and can be kept under control on the steep sidehill sections.

Beyond the end of the trail there is good access to the main ridges of Rocher Deboule Range. Experienced mountain hikers and climbers can easily effect link-ups with Chicago Creek Trail [RD4] and Station Creek Trail [RD5].

PANGEA CREEK TRAIL [RD7]

(Route map on p.94)

LOCATION:
Rocher Deboule Range, near Hazelton.

MAPS REQUIRED:
93M/3 Moricetown (1:50,000)
93M/4 Skeena Crossing (1:50,000)
93M Hazelton (1:250,000)

ROUTE DESCRIPTION:
Approximately 5 km from start of trail at elevation 650 m to semi-open country at 1150 m. A fair trail, reasonably well defined, that is initially an overgrown logging road across a clear-cut area. It stays close to the true left bank of Mudflat Creek and after 1.5 km enters standing timber. Almost immediately it crosses a small creek. Shortly thereafter the skid-road ends and becomes a trail that continues along Mudflat Creek for another kilometer or so to elevation 900 m where it crosses the creek. A very small tributary joins Mudflat Creek from the south at that point. The trail on the other side of Mudflat Creek starts off by following the true left bank of the tributary for a short distance and then bears right away from it, first over fairly flat ground, and then more steeply up the hillside. That part of the trail is not well defined and some care is required to avoid losing it. Should that happen, set a course due south to eventually intersect Pangea Creek and find the trail well above the creek on the true right bank.

The trail beyond Mudflat Creek improves after a 1/2 km or so as soon as it leaves the valley bottom. As it climbs quite steeply across the slope, it crosses a couple of minor streams and the intervening ridges. Pangea Creek comes within earshot near elevation 1000 m and thereafter, for about the last kilometer, the trail does not deviate far from the creek.

At elevation 1150 m are the remains of a camp on the edge of an open slide area and the trail comes to an end. It is still possible to find parts of the trail that at one time continued to the 1400 m level on the west side of the creek, where Lone Star claim was located. However, from the old camp, it is easy enough to reach open country by simply following the creek up and it is not worth looking for the trail.

Allow a good 2 hours up to the old camp and an hour or so down.

DIRECTIONS:
Proceed as for Blue Lake Trail [RD6], but at the signpost, **where the clear-cut begins**, keep left instead of turning up the hill. The alder that has grown up along the road has been partly cleared, so it is not too difficult to get along. There is very little change in elevation as the road follows Mudflat Creek to the edge of the standing timber straight ahead.

COMMENTS:

The trail itself is not of great interest nor does it lead to any significant destination, however, it does provide good access to the open ridge south of Blue Lake which in turn connects with the spine of Rocher Deboule Range. It would be of interest to anyone looking for easy access to the head of Porphyry Creek. Some maintenance has been carried out from time to time, so the trail is in quite good condition.

Resting above Blue Lake.

BOULDER CREEK ROAD [RD8]

LOCATION:
Rocher Deboule Range, near Hazelton.

MAPS REQUIRED:
93M/3 Moricetown (1:50,000)
93M/4 Skeena Crossing (1:50,000)
93M Hazelton (1:250,000)

DIRECTIONS:
About 25 km east of Hazelton and almost the same distance from Smithers along Hwy.16, the road crosses Boulder Creek bridge. Just beyond the bridge, when travelling towards Smithers, Boulder Creek Road branches off to the right (westerly). Almost immediately it passes under a powerline and starts to climb. For the first couple of kilometers, to about elevation 700 m, the road is in fair condition and not unduly steep, but then it becomes very rough and muddy and much steeper. Over the next 2 km it climbs to 900 m where the road improves somewhat as it starts to drop down again. After another 2 km or so, the road is back down to elevation 750 m and following the true right bank of Boulder Creek. It continues along the creek with very little gain in elevation to where the creek forks about 2 km farther upstream and then for another kilometer follows the south fork of Boulder Creek. The road then leaves the creek and for the next 3 km climbs up the open hillside on switchbacks to the remains of a mining camp near the top. Beyond the camp, the road continues on to a small plateau where it reaches an elevation of 1500 m and ends, nearly 15 km from the highway.

COMMENTS:
It may be of interest to some that the name Straw Creek was used instead of Boulder Creek on older map editions and therefore, this road was previously referred to as Straw Creek Road.

Most standard vehicles should be be able to negotiate the first 2 km, but even 4-wheel drive vehicles have trouble getting much beyond that except under the most favourable conditions. The best form of transportation is a mountain bike. It is a great improvement on hiking along what for the most part can only be described as a long and tedious road. The exception is the switchback portion where the country is open and the views get better all the way as the road quickly gains elevation. As it happens, the road surface is also far too rough for anything but walking there.

At the end of the road, 2400 m Tiltusha Peak, second highest in Rocher Deboule Range, looms up impressively across an equally impressive basin. A sharp ridge, which is the spine of the range, continues south from Tiltusha and leads directly to Brian Boru Peak, which at 2500 m, is the highest point in

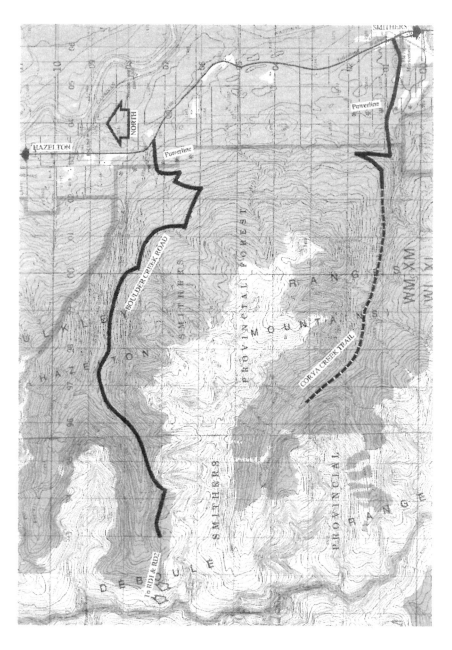

BOULDER CREEK ROAD [RD8]
CORYA CREEK TRAIL [RD9]
(Part of Maps 93M/3&4)
1cm=1km, 100ft.(30m) contour interval

the range. Boulder Creek Road is the most obvious access route to both Tiltusha and Brian Boru Peaks from the east. Various lesser peaks and ridges are also accessible and there are some lovely places to camp near the end of the road, in spite of the mess left behind by mineral exploration activities.

It is possible to link up with either Juniper Creek Road [RD1] or Brian Boru Trail [RD2] by crossing over the main ridge just south of Tiltusha Peak. Another possibility is to head south across the divide between Boulder and Corya Creeks to link up with Corya Creek Trail [RD9].

Looking back down Boulder Creek towards Blunt Mountain.

**Tiltusha Peak from Boulder Creek Road;
route across range is through saddle.**

CORYA CREEK TRAIL [RD9]
(Route map on p.102)

LOCATION:
Rocher Deboule Range, near Smithers.

MAPS REQUIRED:
93M/3 Moricetown (1:50,000)
93M/4 Skeena Crossing (1:50,000)
93M Hazelton (1:250,000)

ROUTE DESCRIPTION:
From start of trail at southeast corner of logged area, elevation 750 m, to open country at 1100 m on north fork of Corya Creek, is a distance of about 10 km. For the first kilometer or so, there is virtually no trail. What used to be a passable skid road following the southern boundary of the logged area is now completely overgrown. However, by fighting through the underbrush, it is possible to eventually reach the southwest corner of the cut block. From there, the trail initially bears slightly right as it drops down somewhat, but it soon returns to a heading of almost due west. For the next couple of kilometers, there is practically no change in elevation as the trail gradually approaches Corya Creek. It is reasonably well defined most of the way, but overgrown and difficult to follow across some open areas. In places it is very muddy and there are many windfalls. Just before reaching Corya Creek, the trail crosses the first significant tributary.

After following the true left (north) bank of the creek for almost a kilometer, the trail crosses to the other side and follows it upstream for a kilometer or so. At a point where the south bank has caved in and not far downstream from where Corya Creek forks, the trail returns to the north bank. If the creek is at all high, it may be just as easy to remain on the north side and follow the ill defined track that exists there most of the way.

The trail continues up the north fork of Corya Creek, but is in poor condition and difficult to follow. In some places it is easier going up the creek bed than to find a route through the fairly thick bush.

Allow 5-6 hours hiking to reach open country and not much less to get back.

DIRECTIONS:
Heading west towards Hazelton, Hwy.16 crosses the railway on an overpass at Moricetown. Just beyond it and about 35 km from Smithers, turn onto the road going left immediately after the gas station. The road goes through private property and less than 2 km from the highway there is a gate, so permission is required to continue. Right after the gate, the road goes under a powerline. Keep going in more or less the same direction until about 3 km from the highway, then look for a somewhat overgrown road heading

Brian Boru from head of Corya Creek.

up the hill to the right. As it climbs, the old logging road makes a long traverse out to the right, but eventually it heads back to the left. At elevation 750 m and some 6 km from the highway, the road turns to the right again and continues to climb. Leave the road there and take the badly overgrown skid road straight ahead. It intersects the southeast corner of the logged off area in less than half a kilometer.

The road is passable for standard vehicles for the first 3 km to the base of the hill and for some distance beyond that with 4-wheel drive. It is not a particularly steep or rough road, but it is really too badly overgrown to be suitable for anything but walking.

COMMENTS:

Because the road access is not very good and the trail itself is long and tedious as well as being in poor condition, it is of only limited interest. It does provide a direct, relatively quick access and exit route to/from Brian Boru Peak, which at 2500 m is the highest summit in Rocher Deboule Range. The basin at the head of Corya Creek is very spectacular with some massive moraines left by the major glacier on the east flank of Brian Boru and surmounting it all, the great peak itself. From the basin, there is a fair route across the ridge to the north, so it is quite possible to exit via Boulder Creek Road [RD8].

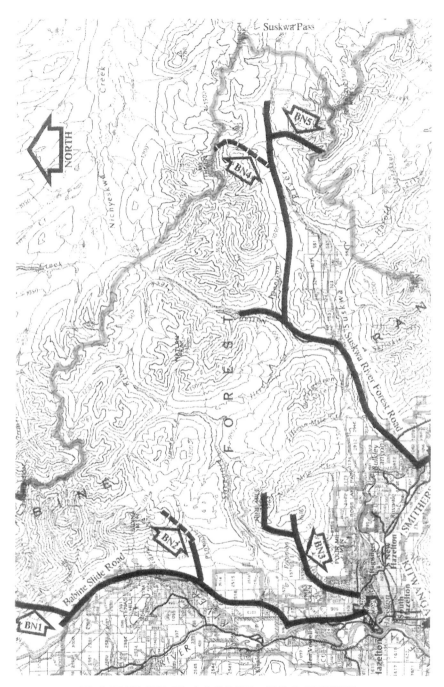

BABINE RANGE (NORTH)

1cm=3.3km, 150m contour interval

BABINE RANGE (NORTH)

From the point of view of access, it is convenient to divide the Babine Range into a North and a South section with the dividing line following first the Suskwa River then Harold Price Creek southeast towards Babine Lake. Otherwise there is little to distinguish the northern from the southern section of the range, so the notes relating to Babine Range (South), in general, apply to the northern section as well.

Access to the northern section is primarily via forestry and mining roads heading north and east from Hazelton. It is also possible to approach from Babine Lake on the east side of the range, but it is a long, roundabout route except when aiming for French Peak. There is road access to claims on French Peak from Smithers via the north end of Babine Lake.

The history of the northern section is also closely connected with Hazelton and is largely covered by the notes relating to Rocher Deboule Range. It is interesting to note, however, that the old Babine Trail from Hazelton to Babine Lake crosses the range here. From Hazelton it follows first the Bulkley and then the Suskwa River upstream. At the head of the latter, it crosses a low (1000 m) pass and drops down to Babine Lake, more or less following Tsezakwa Creek.

The trail was rebuilt under a government contract in 1871 to improve access from the west via Hazelton to the Omineca gold fields. It was a well established native trading route long before that, used by the Babine Indians in their dealings with the Tsimpsians along the Skeena (21).

Hudson's Bay Company in 1822 had established a fort (Kilmaurs) farther south on Babine Lake, but in about 1840 they attempted to start a new one right where the Babine Trail hits the lake. Fort Babine, as it was called, was intended to channel the trade along the Babine Trail through Hudson's Bay Company instead of through the Indians. The fishing was also exceptionally good there and fish was an important source of food for the Company's employees just as it was for the natives. As might be expected, this move on the part of Hudson's Bay Company to muscle in led to hostilities and eventually Fort Babine was abandoned.

One of a relatively small number of mines in West Central British Columbia that have actually operated successfully is Silver Standard on Glen Mountain, just north of Hazelton. The property was originally staked in 1910 and the first shipments of ore containing gold, silver, lead and zinc were made in 1913. Since that time, the mine has been in operation on and off. Some ore has also come out of various claims on Nine Mile Mountain, about 12 km to the northeast of Glen Mountain. For a couple of years from 1927 to 1929, a small mill was in operation at the Silver Cup group of claims on Nine Mile Mountain, but the venture was found to be unprofitable (19).

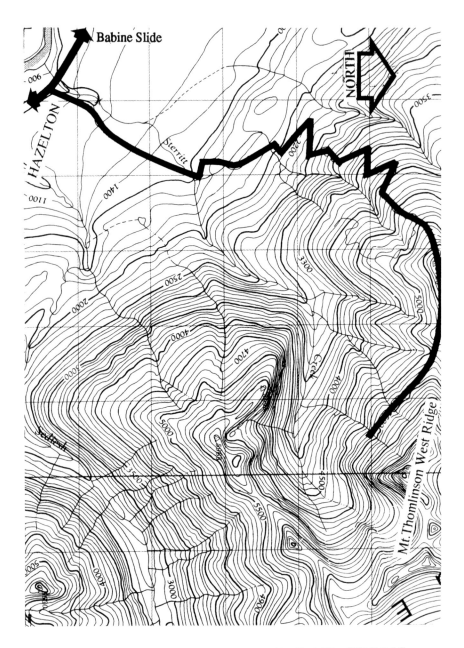

MT. THOMLINSON ROAD [BN1]

(Part of Map 93M/12)

1cm=1/2km, 100ft.(30m) contour interval

MT. THOMLINSON ROAD [BN1]

LOCATION:
Babine Range (North), near Hazelton.

MAPS REQUIRED:
93M/5 Hazelton (1:50,000)
93M/12 Kisgegas (1:50,000)
93M Hazelton (1:250,000)

DIRECTIONS:
At New Hazelton, turn north off Hwy.16 and follow the road to (Old) Hazelton for about 6 km. Turn right onto Kispiox Valley Road and after 3 km turn right again onto Salmon River Road. At Shegunia River bridge, about 9 km from the turn-off, is km 0 of Babine Slide Forest Service Road, which is a continuation of Salmon River Road. Cross Sediesh Creek at km 19, but just before Sterritt Creek near km 21, turn right onto a somewhat overgrown side road. It basically follows Sterritt Creek upstream and then crosses the creek just over 2 km from the turn-off. In that stretch of road there are two forks, keep right at the first and left at the next one. After crossing Sterritt Creek, the road traverses a logged-off area for the next couple of kilometers, at first bearing left and crossing a tributary stream and then turning right again and heading northerly towards the upper boundary of the cutblock. To that point the road is in fair condition and just passable for standard vehicles, but once in the standing timber, it is so badly overgrown with alder as to be virtually impassable except on foot. That continues for the next 3 km as the road switchbacks up the steep hillside. Above the alder belt, the road becomes better again, but in places very steep. The remains of a mining camp can still be found at the 1350 m level and at 1500 m, some 9 km from the Babine Slide Road, the road reaches semi-alpine country. The high point of the road, nearly 1700 m, comes after another kilometer. The road goes on, but starts to drop again as it circles to the right around the head of a basin.

COMMENTS:
This road provides access to the long, west ridge of Mt. Thomlinson, but the main 2440 m peak is still 10 km or so farther east and along the ridge are several lesser peaks.

Because Mt. Thomlinson occupies a strategic position at the north end of the Babine Range and is separated from adjacent ranges by major valleys, there are outstanding views in all directions.

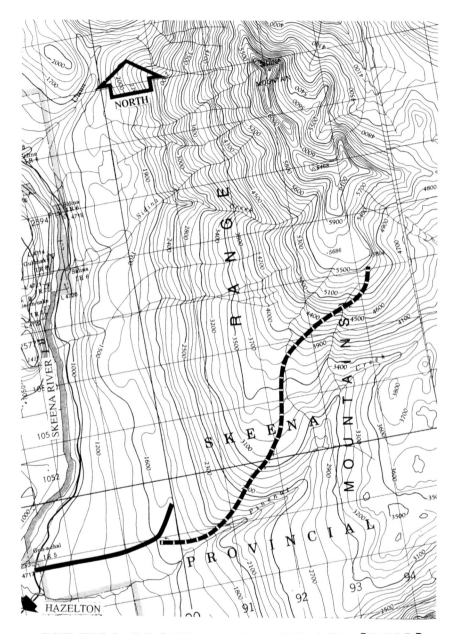

SIDINA MOUNTAIN TRAIL [BN2]

(Part of Maps 93M/5&6)

1cm=2/3km, 100ft.(30m) contour interval

110

SIDINA MOUNTAIN TRAIL [BN2]

LOCATION:
Babine Range (North), near Hazelton.

MAPS REQUIRED:
93M/5 Hazelton (1:50,000)
93M/6 Suskwa River (1:50,000)
93M Hazelton (1:250,000)

ROUTE DESCRIPTION:
　　About 7 km from end of road near southeast corner of logged area, elevation 500 m, to top end of trail at 1600 m. The trail is joined where the southeast corner of the cut-block comes very close to a tributary to Pinenut Creek. From there the trail follows the true right (north) bank of the creek for a good kilometer before crossing to the other side and then leaving the creek. For the next couple of kilometers it climbs through the timber, out of contact with any significant creeks, but gradually approaching the north fork of Pinenut Creek. After following the true right (west) bank of the creek for a short distance, the trail crosses to the other side at about elevation 1100 m. Just before the crossing, there are several old campsites. At the first one, there is a branch trail to the right that goes across the creek, but it simply amounts to an alternative creek crossing, since the trail on the other side heads up the same slope as the main trail. Once over the creek, the trail heads up and across the slope towards the more easterly branch of Pinenut Creek. It crosses that creek at about elevation 1400 m and then follows the true left bank quite closely before eventually petering out near elevation 1600 m.

　　Allow 2-3 hours hiking to reach timberline and almost an hour less to get back.

DIRECTIONS:
　　Proceed from New Hazelton as for Mt. Thomlinson Road [BN1], but stay on Babine Slide Forest Service Road to only just beyond the crossing of Pinenut Creek at about km 5. Turn onto the side road going right less than a kilometer after Pinenut Creek. Depending on conditions and the vehicle used, it may be passable for up to 4 km to elevation 500 m. Pick the best route from there across the slash to the southeast corner of the cut-block.

COMMENTS:
　　This is quite an old trail, dating back to before 1911, when it was put in to service the Silverton group of claims located at the 1400 m level on what was then called Cariboo Mountain. Some work has been done from time to

Sidina Mountain from south side of Pinenut Creek.

time to keep the trail open, but for the last few years, judging by the number of windfalls, it has been rather neglected. However, most of the way it is not hard to follow and it does lead to a large and attractive alpine area. With a better trail through the timber, it would also be a very attractive back-country ski area.

The strategic location occupied by Sidina Mountain means that the views are great in all directions and particularly to the southwest of Rocher Deboule and the Seven Sisters.

NINE MILE MOUNTAIN ROAD [BN3]

LOCATION:
Babine Range (North), near Hazelton.

MAPS REQUIRED:
93M/5 Hazelton (1:50,000)
93M/6 Suskwa River (1:50,000)
93M Hazelton (1:250,000)

DIRECTIONS:
Turn north off Hwy.16 at New Hazelton and follow the road to (Old) Hazelton for close to 4 km, crossing the Bulkley River on the suspension bridge at Hagwilget Canyon on the way. At the village of Two Mile, turn right onto 2nd Avenue. Keep left on Nine Mile Mountain/Silver Standard Road at the first fork and left again at the next fork, about 2 km farther a-long. The road then climbs up a small hill and after just over a kilometer comes to another fork. Take the right branch that drops down and crosses Two Mile Creek. Shortly thereafter, keep right again at the next fork and continue on for about 4 km. At that point, some 8 km from the Old Hazelton road, look for a turn-off to the right and start climbing very steeply uphill. The road goes right to the top of Nine Mile Mountain. In places the grade is extreme and the surface very rough, but with 4-wheel drive it is just possible to get up.

After climbing about 3 km to near timberline at 1300 m, there is a fork in the road. To the right the road leads to a microwave repeater installation, just over a kilometer away on the south summit, at elevation 1600 m. The other branch first heads northerly for 2-3 km and then westerly as it circles a-round the basin where Nine Mile Creek starts. It eventually passes to the north of the main, 1800 m summit of Nine Mile Mountain and drops down onto the long southeast ridge, where it goes to various mineral exploration sites.

COMMENTS:
From some points on the road along the southeast ridge, it is possible to catch a glimpse of another road down below on the steep north slope of the mountain. It is the end of the road that continues straight ahead at the fork 8 km from Old Hazelton road. It was the access to Silver Cup mill and the mine workings beyond. From the end of the road at 1400 m, access to the ridge is fairly easy, so that a link up with Nine Mile Mountain Road is quite feasible. As a matter of fact, by mountain bike or on skis, the old Silver Cup road could provide the easiest access because it was built to avoid severe grades. That also makes it a longer route to timberline, of course. Once up, the alpine area is quite extensive and the terrain ideal for skiing. There is

**Looking north from Nine Mile Mountain
towards Sidina Mountain and Mt. Thomlinson.**

enough road above timberline to make it an attractive area for mountain biking as well.

Except when viewed from the north, Nine Mile Mountain is rather insignificant. However, it is strategically located with respect to several major valleys and adjacent ranges, so there are very impressive views in all directions. In particular, the view of Rocher Deboule, looming massively across the Bulkley River to the south, is outstanding.

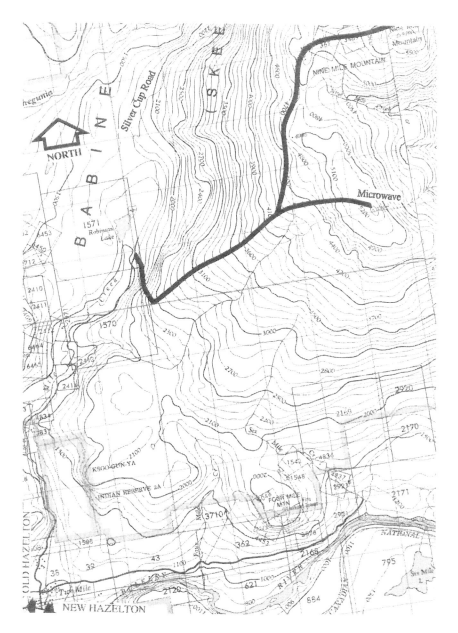

NINE MILE MOUNTAIN ROAD [BN3]

(Part of Maps 93M/5&6)

1cm=2/3km, 100ft.(30m) contour interval

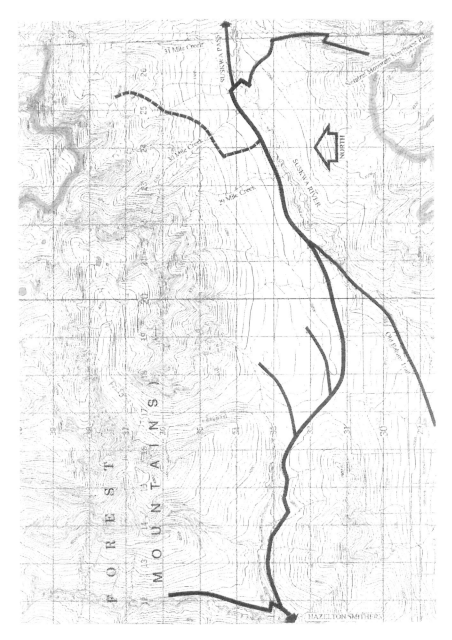

THOEN BASIN TRAIL [BN4]
NETALZUL MOUNTAIN ROAD [BN5]
(Part of Maps 93M/6&7)
1cm=1km, 100ft.(30m) contour interval

116

THOEN BASIN TRAIL [BN4]

LOCATION:
Babine Range (North), near Hazelton.

MAPS REQUIRED:
93M/6 Suskwa River (1:50,000)
93M Hazelton (1:250,000)

ROUTE DESCRIPTION:
   Approximately 6 km from start of trail, elevation 900 m, to timberline at 1500 m on the ridge between Thoen and True Fissure Basins. Although the trail is ill defined in some places, particularly for the first couple of kilometers, and there are many windfalls and muddy sections, it is not unduly difficult to follow. Blaze marks and saw-cut logs help to locate the trail. As an additional aid to navigation, it is worth noting that the trail fairly consistently maintains a heading of due north magnetic, with only brief deviations to either side.
   It is a somewhat tedious trail without any views until timberline is reached. To start with it climbs very slowly and at 30 Mile Creek, just before the half way point, the trails drops nearly 50 m to cross the creek before climbing steeply up the other side. After that, it gains elevation more quickly and as it does, the trail gets better.
   Allow 3-4 hours hiking to reach timberline and 2-3 hours to get back.

DIRECTIONS:
   Going east from New Hazelton on Hwy.16, turn left off the highway after 12 km, just beyond a railway overpass, onto Suskwa River Forest Road. The sign identifying the road also marks km 0. From the bottom of the hill, the road follows the Bulkley River downstream for a short distance before crossing it. At km 15, cross the Suskwa River and follow the main road to the right. It crosses Natlan Creek soon after and then heads up a long hill. Turn right off the main road onto Denison Road at km 21. Shortly after the 5 km marker, turn right onto Thoen Main. Within sight of the km 10 marker of that road, between two clear-cuts, there is a signpost at the edge of the timber on the left marking the start of Thoen Basin Trail.
   It may be possible to drive all the way to the trail head with a standard vehicle, however, it is mainly a winter logging road, so it could be too soft for even 4-wheel drive.

**Thoen Mountain as seen from Netalzul Mountain Road;
30 Mile Creek is on the far left.**

COMMENTS:

Although the trail is not good, it does provide reasonable access to some impressive basins and ridges and ultimately to the 2300 m summit of Thoen Mountain. The Thoen massif stands somewhat isolated, so the views are outstanding in all directions. Except to the east, logging roads follow the base all the way round, which makes it possible to contemplate various interesting traverses. In particular, the northwest ridge appears to offer a fairly easy route down to the road that passes over the saddle between Natlan Creek and Nichyeskwa Creek.

It is interesting to note the reason for creek names such 29 Mile, 30 Mile and so on. The mileages indicate distances from Hazelton along the historic Babine Trail. For the last couple of kilometers, the Denison access road coincides with the Babine Trail that came up the Suskwa River and continued through Suskwa Pass to the north end of Babine Lake.

NETALZUL MOUNTAIN ROAD [BN5]
(Route map on p.116)

LOCATION:
Babine Range (North), near Hazelton.

MAPS REQUIRED:
93M/6 Suskwa River (1:50,000)
93M/7 Netalzul Mountain (1:50,000)
93M Hazelton (1:250,000)

DIRECTIONS:

Proceed as for Thoen Basin Trail [BN4], but continue on along Thoen Main across 30 Mile Creek. There, just before km 11, turn right onto Grizzly Main which heads down and across Suskwa River. On the far side, the road switchbacks up and emerges into another clear-cut where it follows the true right bank of a small creek upstream. Keep right at the fork about 1½ km along Grizzly Main and cross the stream. Leave the logging road there and join Netalzul Mountain Road as it follows the true left bank of the creek up into
the standing timber. At that point, a kilometer or so from the Suskwa, the elevation is close to 950 m. From there, the road climbs to timberline at 1300 m over a distance of 2-3 km, following the true left bank of the creek quite closely most of the way. In a couple of places, the road crosses briefly to the other side of the creek, but none of the crossings are difficult. Half way up are the remains of an old mining camp and beyond that, the road starts to switchback up some steeper sections.
Although the road continues for some distance above timberline, it soon becomes ill defined and difficult to follow. It is easier then to pick a route along the valley and gradually up onto the northwest ridge to the right.

COMMENTS:
On the way up the northwest ridge, several old mine shafts can be seen across the valley to the east. Prospecting and exploration first occurred prior to 1917 and resulted in the Higgins Group of claims. The road is of relatively recent origin and replaced the original pack-trail.
Netalzul Mountain stands somewhat isolated and there are superb views from the 2350 m summit and also from other points on the ridge, lower down. To the east is a great panorama with Babine Lake as the centrepiece. To the south is the impressive northern aspect of Mount Cronin and other peaks in the Babine Mountains Recreation Area. The Thoen massif dominates the scene to the north across the Suskwa and directly to the west, Blunt Mountain stands out against a background of other great ranges.
To the south and southwest, the Upper Fulton Forest Service Road

119

follows the base of Netalzul Mountain quite closely, thus creating opportunities for some interesting traverses.

Where the Denison access road turns right, just before crossing the Suskwa, the Babine Trail continues on along the north side of the river for at least another 10 km before it reaches Suskwa Pass. On the east side, logging roads cover the 15 km or so from the north end of Babine Lake almost right up to the pass, so on skis or even with a mountain bike, it is quite possible to follow most of the historic route linking Hazelton and Babine Lake.

Netalzul Mountain; road leads to ridge on the right.

BABINE RANGE (SOUTH)

The Babine Range extends for 150 km from the junction of the Skeena and Babine Rivers in the northwest to the junction of the Bulkley and Morice Rivers in the southeast. At its widest, the range covers 60 km from Hazelton to the north end of Babine Lake. The highest peak, Mt.Thomlinson in the northwest corner of the range, reaches an elevation of nearly 2450 m. Because it is cut by several low valleys, the Babine Range is not readily perceived as a continuous range, but rather as an assembly of isolated mountains.

For the purpose of access, the range has been divided into a North and a South section, with the dividing line following first the Suskwa River then Harold Price Creek southeast towards Babine Lake. Access and a few other features unique to the northern section, are dealt with under Babine Range (North), but for the most part, these notes apply equally to both sections.

The two major peaks of Babine Range (South), Mt.Cronin (2380 m) and Mt.Hyland (2290 m), are centrally located. A spur projecting westerly from Mt.Cronin terminates with Lagopus Mountain (2130 m). All around the central massif, the range flattens out into a plateau-like landscape broken here and there by depressions and minor peaks.

Access to the southern section of the Babine Range is exceptionally good. Starting from Smithers, there is a wide choice of roads and trails leading into the range from both the east and the west. That, in combination with the large areas of gentle, alpine terrain, with countless small lakes and streams, surrounding the central core of rugged peaks, makes it perhaps the best hiking and ski-touring country to be found anywhere in West Central British Columbia. The outstanding characteristics of the range have been officially recognized by its designation as Babine Mountains Recreation Area. As such it is administered by the Parks Branch and receives some special attention and a certain amount of protection.

GEOGRAPHICAL FEATURES

Sedimentary and volcanic rocks of the Hazelton group are the main building blocks of the range. Those rocks are invaded by granodiorite stocks (Bulkley intrusions) in several locations. The intrusions, probably related to the batholithic rocks of the Coast Mountains 60 km or so to the west, are significant because of the mineral deposits frequently associated with them.

A few minor glaciers that still remain on the north-facing slopes of Mt.Hyland and Mt.Cronin, appear to be retreating. Small alpine lakes have formed behind many of the terminal moraines left by the receding glaciers. The large number of lakes in this range is quite remarkable.

The deep canyons cut by many of the creeks and the flat-topped spurs left projecting out between them are very notable features. The spurs between Cronin, Higgins and Little Joe Creeks and between Reiseter and Harold Price Creeks are most striking. Ganokwa Creek has carved out the most

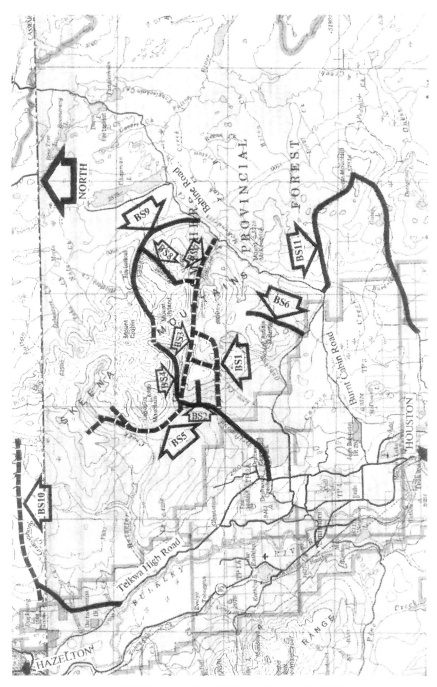

BABINE RANGE (SOUTH)

1cm=3.3km, 500ft.(150m) contour interval

impressive canyon, seen to its best advantage from Burnt Cabin Road. Where Driftwood Creek has cut through soft, sedimentary rocks to form Driftwood Canyon, extensive fossil beds are exposed and fine specimens of plant and animal fossils can be found in the talus. The area is a Provincial Park with day use facilities.

Timberline is generally close to 1500 m. Below that elevation, except where fire or clear-cut logging has destroyed the timber, the slopes are well covered with spruce, balsam and poplar.

Both the major access routes, Babine Lake Road and Driftwood Creek Road, reach elevations of about 900 m. At that level and above, the undergrowth in many places is quite light and it may be fairly easy to travel through the bush without any trail. However, windfalls are bad in unpredictable places, so without a trail, progress can be very much slower than expected.

Since the Babine Range covers a large area and to the north and east merges into virtually unpopulated wilderness, it is prime habitat for the larger mammals. However, the southern section is somewhat isolated from the rest of the range and almost surrounded by farmland and clear-cuts. It has been extensively prospected and explored over a long period of time. For those reasons, the caribou have vanished from the range. There are conflicting reports about when that happened. Some put the date as early as 1907 while others say caribou were seen there as late as 1942. Now the only sign that they once inhabited the range is the occasional discarded antler slowly rotting away. Until a few years ago, when hunting was severely restricted, it seemed that the mountain goat population was going the same way, but lately there has been an encouraging reversal of that trend.

Moose are frequently seen, as are black bears, and in recent years, deer. It is unlikely that there are many resident grizzly bears, but they certainly pass through the area on their wanderings and are occasionally seen. Coyotes are a common sight, particularly on the fringes of the range. Wolves, wolverines, lynx and smaller furbearing animals are seldom seen, but are by no means rare. There is a healthy population of marmots and, cyclically, of lemmings, above timberline. Porcupines and squirrels are encountered more frequently than any other mammals at lower elevations. Grouse and ptarmigan are common as are all other species of birds normally found in the latitudes and climatic zones represented.

MINING

One area in particular has been extensively prospected and mined since 1909 when James Cronin secured claims on Tuchi River, now Cronin Creek. The principal property was Bonanza and in 1910 James Cronin formed the Bonanza Mining and Milling Company to develop it. There were then three trails to the property: one from Telkwa, another via Driftwood Creek and a third starting at Moricetown and coming in from the north. In 1916 access was much improved when a sleigh road and later a waggon road was built from Telkwa with government assistance. Small scale mining and milling has been carried on intermittently, by various operators, through the years, to the present. Lead and zinc concentrates have been the main products of the operation with silver, cadmium and gold as byproducts.

Most of the mineral deposits of any significance are concentrated in close proximity to Mts.Cronin and Hyland. Those deposits have led to construction of the numerous roads and trails that now provide such good access to the range for recreational purposes.

On the negative side, indiscriminate exploration with heavy equipment has left some ugly scars, particularly on the southwest slopes of Astlais Mountain and to a lesser extent on Harvey Mountain. The activity in Silver King Basin, has fortunately been confined to a small area, mostly underground, so the damage done is minor. That is also the case in the Cronin Creek area, but the damage there is more extensive. The damage in those areas should heal in a relatively short time since it is at or below timberline, in sheltered locations, where nature is amazingly efficient at obliterating man-made scars. Any future exploration within the Babine Mountains Recreation Area will hopefully be tightly controlled by the Parks Branch and therefore less destructive.

HISTORICAL NOTES

The history of the southern section of the Babine Range is part of the history of Bulkley Valley and is covered in the notes pertaining to Hudson Bay Range. In addition, it is of interest to note that the southwestern foothills of the Babine Range, from Driftwood Creek to Telkwa, was among the first areas in the Bulkley Valley to be settled.

FUTURE PROSPECTS

As its history, so also its future, is closely tied to that of the Bulkley Valley and the Hudson Bay Range and the same comments generally apply. With Smithers and the Bulkley Valley becoming increasingly popular as destinations for an emerging breed of tourists that seek active outdoor recreation pursuits, such as hiking, climbing and ski touring, and as local residents in greater numbers turn to such activities, the Babine Range, and particularly the southern section, will become widely recognized as an outstanding recreation area. To maintain and enhance the characteristics that make it so, while at the same time utilizing such a valuable recreational resource for the maximum benefit of the local economy, is going to be a challenging resource mananagement exercise.

Designation by the government of the Babine Mountains Recreation Area indicates some official recognition of the value of this priceless asset. In recent years, the Parks Branch has made some encouraging moves towards both protection and enhancement of the area. With more public support, their management activities should become less tentative and more visible.

LYON CREEK TRAIL [BS1]

LOCATION:
Babine Range (South), Babine Mountains Recreation Area, near Smithers.

MAPS REQUIRED:
93L/15 Driftwood Creek (1:50,000)
93L Smithers (1:250,000)

ROUTE DESCRIPTION:
About 5 km from start of trail on Driftwood Creek at elevation 850 m to timberline at 1450 m. A good, well defined trail on a reasonably easy grade. For the first couple of kilometers, the trail was at one time the access road to a sawmill, but now there is little left of either the road or the sawmill. Beyond the sawmill site, the trail bears right and then left again as it climbs quite steeply for a short distance. The grade eases after that and the only other steep section is the last kilometer or so before the trail reaches timberline. Once out in the open, the trail contours around the southeast flank of Harvey Mountain and then drops down slightly to cross Lyon Creek.

Immediately after the crossing, there is a fork in the trail. The branch to the right heads up a tributary to Lyon Creek, over a 1650 m pass and then down into the wide, open Ganokwa Creek basin. Bearing left again, it skirts a small lake and climbs gently through mostly open country to the divide between the watersheds of Ganokwa, Driftwood and Little Joe creeks. The trail to the left at Lyon Creek fork follows the creek upstream, remaining on the true left bank, except for switching to the other side for a short distance. At the head of the creek, the trail just peters out at about elevation 1600 m.

Allow 2-3 hours to hike up to timberline and at least half an hour less to get down.

DIRECTIONS:
From Smithers, proceed as for Silver King Basin Road [BS4], but about **4 km beyond Driftwood Canyon Park (and half a kilometer beyond the bridge at crossing #4 of Driftwood Creek), turn right off Driftwood** Road onto an overgrown side road, which is the start of the trail. At the top of the first hill, watch for a sharp turn left onto what was the old sawmill access road.

COMMENTS:
With relatively little time and effort, this trail leads to some of the most pleasant hiking country to be found anywhere. Once above timberline there is a marvellous view of the Bulkley Valley. The choice of routes becomes almost infinite and link-ups with the many trails and roads that lead into this part of the range makes possible several interesting round trips. The variat-

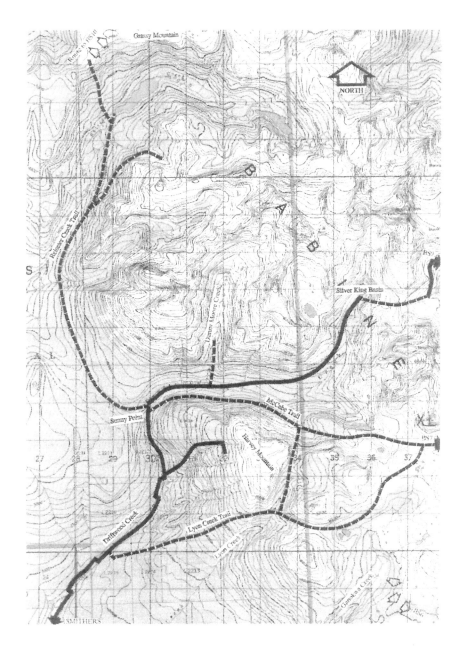

LYON CREEK TRAIL [BS1];HARVEY MOUNTAIN ROAD [BS2]
McCABE TRAIL [BS3];SILVER KING BASIN ROAD [BS4]
REISETER CREEK TRAIL [BS5]
(Part of Maps 93L/14&15)
1cm=1km, 100ft.(30m) contour interval

ions are limited only by the time available and what transportation arrangements can be made.

With only a single vehicle, Harvey Mountain Road [BS2] is the quickest alternate route down. If more time is available, consider returning via McCabe Trail [BS3]. Although the trail up Lyon Creek fades out, it is not difficult to continue on straight ahead through the pass and down the other side to intersect McCabe Trail. From the pass, there is a lovely view across the valley, directly into Silver King Basin and a small lake right at the pass is just the perfect foreground. A sketchy trail does go down the gully beyond the pass, but it fades out before it reaches McCabe Trail. In a long day, a feasible and very enjoyable round trip is to follow the other branch of Lyon Creek Trail to the end where it actually joins McCabe Trail at the base of Mt. Hyland.

A second vehicle makes Onion Mountain Road [BS6], Little Joe Creek Trail [BS7] and Higgins Creek Road [BS8] viable exit routes for long day hikes. If time is available for one or more overnight camps, there is no shortage of lovely places to camp near wood and water almost anywhere in Ganokwa basin. During the short alpine flower season, at its peak in August, the extensive meadows are a riot of colours. The area is home to great colonies of marmots and on the steep, rocky slopes high above the basin, it is not unusual to see mountain goats.

It is interesting to note that Lyon Creek Trail was put in originally to access claims in Victoria Basin at the head of Higgins Creek. Later on Little Joe Creek Trail was used and finally Higgins Creek Road. Considering its origins as a pack trail and the lovely alpine country it leads to, it is not surprising that it is a popular horse trail and that therefore some sections are a bit muddy at times.

Lyon Creek Trail is highly recommended for children and novices since it is not far to timberline and the going is easy. It may seem a bit long and tedious through the timber, but the views higher up more than compensate for persevering. Children's complaints about being tired on the way up are more likely due to boredom and soon forgotten above timberline. On the way down, they will probably run all the way. Keep in mind that on Harvey Mountain water may be hard to find. The first reliable source is Lyon Creek.

HARVEY MOUNTAIN ROAD [BS2]

(Route map on p.126)

LOCATION:
Babine Range (South), Babine Mountains Recreation Area, near Smithers.

MAPS REQUIRED:
93L/15 Driftwood Creek (1:50,000)
93L Smithers (1:250,000)

DIRECTIONS:
From Smithers, proceed as for Silver King Basin Road [BS4], but about 6 km beyond **Driftwood Canyon Park** and just after crossing #6 of Driftwood Creek, take the side road to the right. It switchbacks up the steep mountainside, from 1000 m at the start to 1500 m at timberline, in a distance of 2 km. The road is well laid out and constructed and in quite good condition. Motorized vehicles are not permitted in the Recreation Area, otherwise the road could be negotiated with 4-wheel drive.

COMMENTS:
The road continues on up for a short distance above timberline, then it turns right, crosses Harvey Creek and fades out about a kilometer north of where Lyon Creek Trail [BS1] emerges from the timber. To return via that trail, head slightly up from the end of the road then level off and stay up until far enough along to drop straight down to intersect the trail.

By continuing straight ahead up the slope where the road turns right and levels off, it is quite easy to cross over Harvey Mountain and drop down into the pass at the head of Lyon Creek. From there, both Lyon Creek Trail and McCabe Trail [BS3] are readily accessible.

When snow conditions are favourable, Harvey Mountain Road is a good way to ski down. Other routes or the road can be used to get up. The road is also suitable for horses and mountain bikes.

Babine Mountains; Harvey Mountain is on the right.

128

McCABE TRAIL [BS3]
(Route map on p.126)

LOCATION:
Babine Range (South), Babine Mountains Recreation Area, near Smithers.

MAPS REQUIRED:
93L/15 Driftwood Creek (1:50,000)
93L Smithers (1:250,000)

ROUTE DESCRIPTION:
    About 5.5 km from start of trail by Driftwood Creek (Sunny Point) at elevation 1050 m to timberline at 1500 m. An excellent, well maintained trail on an even, easy grade.

    For a 1/2 km or so follow a rough, steep "cat" road. The trail then veers left away from the road and climbs gently up the steep north slope of Harvey Mountain, roughly parallel to Driftwood Creek. After about 2.5 km and for a distance of 1 km, the trail crosses slide paths covered with slide-alder and other dense vegetation. At times this may overhang and partly obscure the trail, making it slippery and unpleasant when wet. Beyond that section the going is good all the way. Allow 2 hours on the trail up to timberline and 1 to 1.5 hours down.

    Just before timberline, about 4.5 km from Sunny Point and elevation 1400 m, there is an obvious pass to the right (south). A faint branch trail goes up the draw and through the pass where it links up with a branch of Lyon Creek Trail [BS1].

    The main trail continues on above timberline, climbing gently to the divide between Driftwood Creek (south fork) and Little Joe Creek. At the divide, 8 km from Sunny Point and elevation 1700 m, the trail links up with Little Joe Creek Trail [BS7] and passes just below Mt.Hyland (2250 m). Instead of continuing along Little Joe Creek Trail, it is possible to turn south and link up with Lyon Creek Trail [BS1].

    Before the divide, about 6.5 km from Sunny Point, the trail passes close to a chain of three small lakes (Copper Lakes). Ahead are two saddles. The main trail goes through the northerly one. It is also possible to aim for the south saddle and join Lyon Creek Trail that way.

DIRECTIONS:
    From Smithers proceed as for Silver King Basin [BS4], but instead of crossing Driftwood Creek at Sunny Point (7th crossing of Driftwood Creek), turn right onto the "cat" road that goes steeply uphill and follow it for about a 1/2 km. At the end of a short, flattish stretch, the road bears right uphill again. Look for the trail continuing more or less straight ahead and parallel to Driftwood Creek.

COMMENTS:

This is probably the best and easiest trail into the Babine Mountains Recreation Area. The trail goes through open timber at the start and then views open up across and along Driftwood Valley. After about 4 km, the views across the valley into Silver King Basin and ahead to Mt.Hyland are quite spectacular.

Close to and above timberline, there are many fine camping areas. Once above timberline and particularly from the divide between Driftwood and Little Joe Creeks, there is a wide choice of routes and many possibilities for link-ups with other trails (see Lyon Creek Trail [BS1]). There is a lovely view to the east towards Babine Lake with Little Joe Lakes sparkling in the foreground.

The divide is a good point to take off for the summit of Mt.Hyland, which is an easy climb. From the summit, experienced mountain hikers equipped with ice axes can head north, down snowfields and small glaciers, into Hyland Pass and intersect a trail joining Silver King Basin [BS4] and Cronin Creek Road [BS9].

There is no need to traverse Mt.Hyland to reach this trail. McCabe Trail was originally built to provide easy packhorse access, via the east end of Little Joe Lakes and then north through Eagle Pass, to mines at the head of Higgins Creek. The trail remains in good condition all the way there. A road leading down from the old Higgins Creek camp [BS8] joins Cronin Creek Road. Another possibility is to follow a very sketchy trail from the head of Higgins Creek, around the north side of Mt.Hyland, directly to Hyland Pass.

McCabe Trail is highly recommended for children and novices. It provides the easiest and most rewarding access to outstanding hiking and camping areas. For anyone weary and stiff after a long day's hike and a heavy pack, the gentle grade eases the often dreaded descent. It is a good trail for horses and mountain bikes. For skiing it is not recommended mainly because at the outset it traverses the steep north slope of Harvey Mountain. Even when the snow is stable, that part of the trail is quite likely to be filled in with avalanche debris and therefore difficult to ski.

In a dry summer and particularly late in the season, there is little drinking water available below timberline. Higher up that is rarely any problem.

**Silver King Basin
from McCabe Trail.**

SILVER KING BASIN ROAD [BS4]
(Route map on p.126)

LOCATION:
Babine Range (South), Babine Mountains Recreation Area, near Smithers.

MAPS REQUIRED:
93L/14 Smithers (1:50,000)
93L/15 Driftwood Creek (1:50,000)
93L Smithers (1:250,000)

DIRECTIONS:
　　Just after crossing the Bulkley River 3 km east of Smithers on Highway 16, turn left onto Old Babine Lake Road and follow signs to Driftwood Canyon Provincial Park". The road heads up the hill and curves back to overlook Smithers before bearing right and downhill to where it crosses Canyon Creek and the pavement ends 4 km from the highway. After passing Snake Road going off to the left, the main road makes a sharp right turn and starts climbing. In 3 km, at the intersection with Telkwa High Road, turn left and in 2 km turn right onto Driftwood Road, all the while following the "Driftwood Canyon Provincial Park" signs. About 2 km beyond the Park, and shortly after crossing Driftwood Creek for the third time, there is a graded parking area. Beyond that, for the next 6 km or so to Sunny Point, the road is rough, but may be passable most of the way for vehicles with good clearance.

　　After the foot bridge at Sunny Point, take the road going right. It follows Driftwood Creek upstream and remains on the true right side for the next 8 km to the end in Silver King Basin. Over that distance, the elevation increases from 1050 m at Sunny Point to 1450 m.

COMMENTS:
　　Just beyond Sunny Point the road enters Babine Mountains Recreation Area and a gate has been installed there by the Parks Branch to enforce the exclusion of motorized vehicles. By special permits, those who intermittently work the still active mineral claims in Silver King Basin, have always been able to drive vehicles and heavy equipment up and down the road. That means it is generally fairly free of windfalls and brush, but on the other hand it is sometimes rather muddy. There are no very steep sections and the going is easy all the way. It is also somewhat tedious as the road stays in the timber and there are only occasional views.

　　About 2 km beyond Sunny Point, there is a new foot bridge

Entering Silver King Basin.

across Danny Moore Creek. It is a fair sized creek that comes rushing down to join Driftwood Creek from a minor basin between Lagopus Mountain and Axel Peak. There is a sketchy trail up Danny Moore Creek; on the true left bank for the first 2 km and then on the other bank until it peters out after another kilometer or so. It is not of great interest except as an approach route to Lagopus Mountain or as part of a high level alternate route into Silver King Basin via Galleon Ridge and Silver King Lake.

On emerging from the timber at the entrance to Silver King Basin, another fair sized creek cuts across the road. It drains a small, high elevation basin that contains Silver King Lake. To get to it, follow the road for another 1/2 km or so until the slope above offers a reasonable clear route up. Elements of a sketchy trail exist and it is worth looking for to get through some patches of brush high up, near the lake.

Near the back of Silver King Basin, some of the old mining camp buildings are still standing and may be usable. A short distance beyond the camp, the road crosses Driftwood Creek for the last time. It continues to curve around to the right, but very quickly comes to an end. At that point, a trail starts to switchback up the steep slope into Hyland Pass, between Mounts Cronin and Hyland. It is a well constructed pack trail in good condition. On the far side of the pass, it joins up with Cronin Creek Road [BS9] and also with the remains of a trail that continues around the north side of Mt.Hyland into Victoria Basin, at the head of Higgins Creek, where it joins up with Higgins Creek Road [BS8]. From Victoria Basin, a good trail goes through Eagle Pass and links up with Little Joe Creek Trail [BS7], McCabe Trail [BS3] and Lyon Creek Trail [BS1].

Experienced mountain hikers can exit from Silver King Basin via a 2100 m pass to the north and drop down the glacier on the far side. From there it is a spectacular and very pleasant 2-3 day trek back to Sunny Point via the high level plateau (Grassy Mountain) north and west of Reiseter Lakes and Reiseter Creek Trail [BS5].

Silver King Basin has some good camping places and is a convenient starting point for exploration of the surrounding mountains, Cronin and Hyland in particular. The road is well used in the summer by hikers, mountain bikers and horse riders. In the winter it is one of the most popular routes for ski touring. With skis and reasonable snow conditions in the winter or with a mountain bike in the summer, it is possible to coast back down most of the 14 km road.

Perhaps it is a fair measure of its popularity and fame that Silver King Basin Road is the only route in West Central British Columbia to have been included in "The Best of B.C.'s Hiking Trails - Twenty Great Trails" by Bob Harris. As ardent B.C. hikers all know, his excellent write-ups on trails throughout British Columbia used to appear as a regular feature in the magazine BC Outdoors.

REISETER CREEK TRAIL [BS5]
(Route map on p.126)

LOCATION:
Babine Range (South), Babine Mountains Recreation Area, near Smithers.

MAPS REQUIRED:
93L/14 Smithers (1:50,000)
93L/15 Driftwood Creek (1:50,000)
93L Smithers (1:250,000)

ROUTE DESCRIPTION:
About 10 km from the start at Sunny Point, elevation 1050 m, to timberline at 1450 m, near the end of the upper branch of the trail and the same distance to Reiseter Lake, elevation 1200 m, at the end of the lower branch.

The first half of the route is a "cat" track, fairly good for a couple of kilometers while it climbs 100 m or so, then very rough and muddy as it drops right back down again to end at Reiseter Creek. From there, it is a reasonably good trail that has been cleared of windfalls and brush off and on over the years, so the going gets much better. In 2 km the trail climbs to about 1200 m where it forks. To the right is the original prospectors' trail to claims just above timberline. It is well laid out and fairly easy to follow as it climbs gently at first and then more steeply. Near the end are the remains of some old cabins. Beyond that, the trail becomes sketchy, but it is no longer needed since the country is quite open.

The left branch of the trail goes to the lake. It is well used and easy to follow, but it is not so well laid out. There are many steep and muddy ups and downs, some of which could have been avoided. A kilometer or so below the lake, it joins Reiseter Creek and thereafter follows the true left bank upstream.

Just before the trail reaches the lake, there is a branch trail to the left that leads to a ford across the creek. On the other side, a steep, switchback trail has been cut, more or less following an ill defined ridge in a northwesterly direction up to timberline at about 1600 m. It is somewhat sketchy in places and there are many windfalls, but it is a key access route to an extensive and remarkable alpine area, known by some as Grassy Mountain, located west and north of Reiseter Lakes.

DIRECTIONS:
From Smithers, proceed as for Silver King Basin Road [BS4], but at Sunny Point, immediately after the 7th crossing of Driftwood Creek, turn left instead of right.

COMMENTS:
It should be noted that Reiseter Creek and Lake are perhaps better

Looking over Reiseter Lakes towards Mt. Cronin.

known locally by the name Two Bridge.

This is a long and somewhat tedious trail, so it is not recommended for a single day's hike. However, there are some interesting possibilities for those intending to camp out one or more nights. Reiseter Lake has fish in it, so is of great interest to some. There is enough flat ground at the lake for a comfortable camp.

The trail up from the creek to Grassy Mountain opens up unlimited opportunities for hiking, horse riding and camping. It also is the obvious exit route for anyone undertaking the circle tour from Silver King Basin, around to the north of Reiseter Lakes and back to Sunny Point.

At the end of the original pack trail, in the high country southeast of Reiseter Lake, the terrain is much more rugged. The views are great and there is a good chance of seing mountain goats, but the area is likely to be of most interest to experienced mountain hikers who intend to cross the range and exit via Silver King or one of the intermediate basins, such as Danny Moore, on the east side of Lagopus Mountain.

The Grassy Mountain area is ideal terrain for skiing, but at present it is only accessible to those prepared for a long, arduous trip in and out and fully equipped for winter camping.

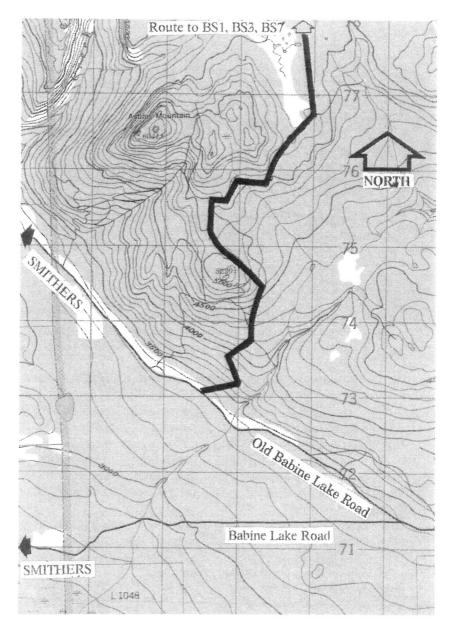

ONION MOUNTAIN ROAD [BS6]

(Part of Map 93L/15)

1cm=1/2km, 100ft.(30m) contour interval

ONION MOUNTAIN ROAD [BS6]

LOCATION:
Babine Range (South), Babine Mountains Recreation Area, near Smithers.

MAPS REQUIRED:
93L/15 Driftwood Creek (1:50,000)
93L Smithers (1:250,000)

DIRECTIONS:
From Smithers, proceed as for Cronin Creek Road [BS9], but just before the 20 km mark, turn sharp left onto what is in fact Old Babine Lake Road. After following it for about 3 km in a northwesterly direction, turn right onto Onion Mountain Road and immediately start climbing steeply up the hillside on a series of switchbacks.

The elevation at the turn-off is just under 1000 m and at timberline, some 3 km farther up the road, it is 1500 m. Beyond timberline, the road continues on for another 5-6 km, to the second of two cabins, without any net gain in elevation.

COMMENTS:
Onion Mountain Road leads to a major, designated snowmobile area, but is closed to other motorized vehicles. The two cabins in the alpine area are operated and maintained by Smithers Snowmobile Association.

There are several other roads, mostly interconnected to some degree, on the southwest slopes of Onion Mountain and adjacent Astlais Mountain. Some of them can be seen quite clearly from below. In fact, the slopes have been so badly scarred, by heavy equipment in the course of intense mineral exploration and by forest fire, as to be something of an eyesore even from a distance. However, Onion Mountain Road in particular provides easy access to the great expanse of open meadows that is Ganokwa Basin and to some magnificent views of the Bulkley Valley and surrounding mountains. While the road is steep in parts below timberline, there are enough gentle slopes and level sections above that a mountain bike makes access even easier.

At the height of the season in August, it is possible to walk for hours through meadows carpeted with alpine flowers by first following the road to the end and then continuing on farther into the basin.

The end of the road is a good starting point for hikes and horse rides to any point in or around Ganokwa Basin. With its many lakes, small streams and patches of timber, the basin has numerous pleasant camping sites. It is very easy to link up with Lyon Creek Trail [BS1], McCabe Trail [BS3] or Little Joe Creek Trail [BS7] at the base of Mount Hyland, some 5 km to the north across the basin.

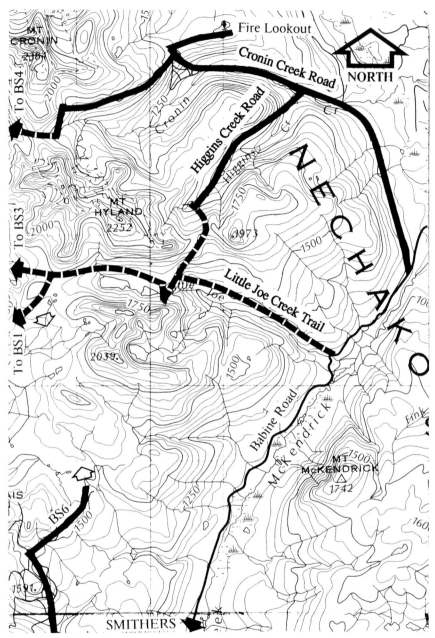

LITTLE JOE CREEK TRAIL [BS7]
HIGGINS CREEK ROAD [BS8]
CRONIN CREEK ROAD [BS9]
(Part of Map 93L/NE)
1cm=1km, 50m contour interval

138

LITTLE JOE CREEK TRAIL [BS7]

LOCATION:
Babine Range (South), Babine Mountains Recreation Area, near Smithers.

MAPS REQUIRED:
93L/15 Driftwood Creek (1:50,000)
93L Smithers (1:250,000)

ROUTE DESCRIPTION:
About 5 km from start of trail on Babine Road, elevation 1000 m, to first lake at 1500 m. It is a good, well maintained trail on a fairly easy grade, most of the way through heavy timber. It remains on the north side of Little Joe Creek all the way up, following the creek quite closely at first and then gradually climbing up the sidehill, away from the creek. Eventually the trail emerges abruptly into an open basin where the trees are small and bushy as a result of occasional avalanche activity. Towards the back of the basin, the trail becomes quite steep and sketchy for a short distance, but continues on without making any change in direction. About half way up the slope, another trail that contours around the basin is intersected. Turn left onto that trail towards Little Joe Creek to get around the steep, top section of the headwall and up into the alpine country above.

The trail does not actually go to either of the two Little Joe Lakes, but continues along well up on the hillside to the north of them. Only when level with the east end of the lower lake, can it be seen some distance below.

Allow 2-3 hours up to the first lake and something less to get down.

DIRECTIONS:
From Smithers, proceed as for Cronin Creek Road [BS9], but at km 30 of Babine Road, immediately after crossing Little Joe Creek, turn left onto a side road that parallels the creek across a cut-block. For almost a kilometer the road is fairly good and climbs gently to a landing near the southwest corner of the cut-block, where there is room to turn around and park.

The start of the trail is well marked. Initially it drops down through the standing timber towards Little Joe Creek, then the trail turns right and follows the creek upstream.

COMMENTS:
The trail was built in 1929 with assistance from the Department of Mines as a shorter access route to claims in Victoria Basin at the head of Higgins Creek. Previously, the only access had been by way of Driftwood, via either Lyon Creek Trail [BS1] or McCabe Trail [BS3]. To link up with either one, simply continue along Little Joe Creek trail to the pass, beyond the west end of the upper lake, at the foot of Mount Hyland. The trail straight ahead

Little Joe Lakes.

through the pass is McCabe Trail. Lyon Creek Trail comes up around the west side of Ganokwa Basin and can be found by turning south off Little Joe Creek Trail just before the pass. It is not easy to pick up the trail without kwowing where to look. If it cannot be found, just head straight for the small lake below the pass leading to Lyon Creek and look for the trail there.

To reach Victoria Basin, it is necessary to turn right instead of left onto the trail intersected at the back of the first open basin on the way up Little Joe Creek Trail. The trail contours around to the north side of the basin and then starts to switcback up towards 1700 m Eagle Pass leading over into Victoria Basin and the top end of Higgins Creek Road [BS8].

The somewhat tedious first few kilometers and the steep, rough section just below the first lake, makes this trail less than ideal for children and for activities other than hiking. However, it does provide quick, direct access from the east to some spectacular country around Little Joe Lakes and opens up exciting possibilities for many interesting cross-over and round trips.

HIGGINS CREEK ROAD [BS8]
(Route map on p.138)

LOCATION:
Babine Range (South), Babine Mountains Recreation Area, near Smithers.

MAPS REQUIRED:
93L/15 Driftwood Creek (1:50,000)
93L Smithers (1:250,000)

DIRECTIONS:
From Smithers, proceed as for Cronin Creek Road [BS9], but shortly after the bridge across Cronin Creek, turn left on a side road to recross the creek, back to the south side. There Higgins Creek joins Cronin Creek. The road climbs from an elevation of 1000 m at the start to nearly 1500 m in Victoria Basin, where it ends a short distance beyond an old mine camp, some 5 km from Cronin Creek. Most of the way, the road follows the true left bank of Higgins Creek, but a kilometer or so from the end, it switches to the other side.

The road is overgrown, but the grade is relatively easy. Motorized vehicles are not permitted. A mountain bike may be a viable alternative.

COMMENTS:
From the end of the road, a good trail continues up to cross the 1700 m saddle straight ahead, which is Eagle Pass. On the other side is the valley of Little Joe Creek where the trail at first drops down perhaps 150 m. It then bears right and contours around to the back of the basin where it joins Little Joe Creek Trail [BS7].

On the way up, the northeast ridge of Mount Hyland is on the right. From the end of the road, an old trail goes over that ridge down into, and then across, Hyland Basin on the far side to eventually link up with the end of Cronin Creek Road. The trail is in poor condition and where it climbs out of Victoria Basin, there is a somewhat hazardous section across a steep sidehill.

The ridge on the southeast side of Higgins Creek is easy to reach from Eagle Pass and offers outstanding views of Babine Lake to the east and north with the Bait Range beyond. Just west of the north end of Babine Lake is French Peak and to the left of it, Netalzul Mountain.

Hiking up Higgins Creek Road is very pleasant. The timber is fairly open and there are good views most of the way. Since it is quite short, not too steep and leads to some interesting remains of past mineral exploration, it is a good hike for children.

Victoria Basin can provide excellent skiing, sometimes well into the spring, but because of the steep slopes, it is well to give careful consideration to avalanche hazards.

141

CRONIN CREEK ROAD [BS9]
(Route map on p.138)

LOCATION:
Babine Range (South), Babine Mountains Recreation Area, near Smithers.

MAPS REQUIRED:
93L/15 Driftwood Creek (1:50,000)
93L Smithers (1:250,000)

DIRECTIONS:
From Smithers, follow Hwy.16 east for about 6 km and turn left onto Babine Lake Road. There is km 0 of that road. After a steady climb

to 1000 m over the first 20 km or so, the road curves to the left as it rounds the shoulder of Onion Mountain, drops slightly and then levels off. Just after the km 32 mark, turn left onto Cronin Creek Road.

For the first 5 km the road heads northerly towards Cronin Creek and then starts to bear left as it approaches the creek. Just over a kilometer farther on, the road crosses to the north side of the creek and follows it upstream for a good 3 km to the site of an old mining camp and mill at elevation 1100 m. The road climbs steeply on a series of switchbacks over the next couple of kilometers to 1800 m on the east ridge of Mount Cronin. It goes on for 2-3 km after that without any further gain in elevation, but drops a 100 m or so at the end, near the head of Cronin Creek, below Hyland Pass.

As far as the bridge across Cronin Creek, the road is just passable with a standard vehicle. A short distance beyond the bridge, the Parks Branch has put up a gate to stop motorized vehicles from entering the Recreation Area.

COMMENTS:
Cronin Creek Road provides good access to the most rugged area of the range. The high point of the road is an obvious place to start an ascent of 2380 m Mount Cronin, the highest peak in the Recreation Area.

On the north and east facing slopes of the bowl at the head of Haystack Creek, the snow stays well into the summer, so it is an area favoured by out-of-season skiers.

From the end of the road, it is an enjoyable hike through Hyland Pass and down into Silver King Basin. Continuing on down the road [BS4] to a second vehicle left on Driftwood Road makes a crossing of the range a feasible, but long day hike and a great ski trip when snow conditions are right. If a mountain bike is used to speed progress beyond the Cronin Creek Road gate, it is not a problem to take it through the pass to exit via Silver King Basin.

Remnants of the old trail from Hyland Basin, at the head of Cronin Creek, across to Higgins Creek in Victoria Basin, can still be found starting from the end of the road. By taking that route, it is possible to link up with Higgins Creek Road [BS8]. From Victoria Basin there is also a good trail up over Eagle Pass that connects with Little Joe Creek Trail [BS7].

On the way up Cronin Creek Road, near the 1500 m level, a side road on the right leads across an intervening saddle to a fire lookout with a fine, panoramic view to the east, including Babine Lake. Just up the road from the turn-off are the remains of some old mine buildings. That is where the original access trail from Moricetown ended. The trail can still be followed with some difficulty, but is badly overgrown and obstructed by windfalls. Some 25 km away to the northwest, as the crow flies, on the far side of the range, part of that trail is still well used, primarily to access the high country west of Harold Price Basin [BS10].

Hyland Basin with Cronin Creek Road; Mt. Cronin on the left.

Mt. Hyland from above Silver King Basin.

143

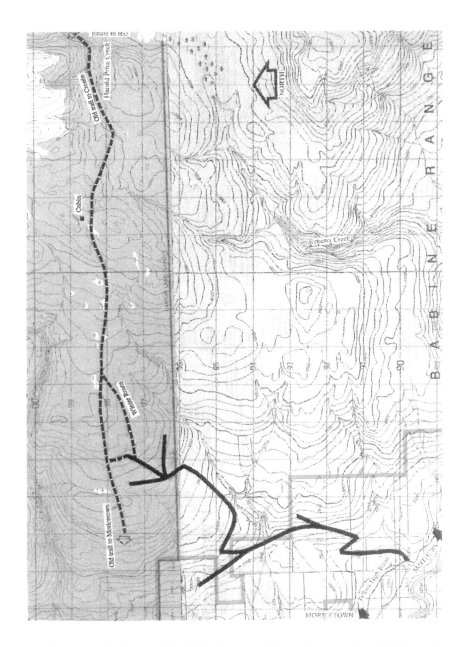

HAROLD PRICE BASIN TRAIL [BS10]

(Part of Maps 93L/14 & 93M/3)

1cm=1km, 100ft.(30m) contour interval

144

HAROLD PRICE BASIN TRAIL [BS10]

LOCATION:
Babine Range (South), near Smithers.

MAPS REQUIRED:
93L/14 Smithers (1:50,000)
93M/3 Moricetown (1:50,000)
93L Smithers (1:250,000)
93M Hazelton (1:250,000)

ROUTE DESCRIPTION:
From the start, where the logging road ends at elevation 1100 m, to semi-alpine meadows at 1450 m on the plateau west of Harold Price Basin, is a distance of about 7 km.

At the end of the road, continue straight across the cut-block and 100 m or so into the standing timber to intersect the trail. The trail is excellent as it climbs to and then follows the crest of the ridge between Gramaphone and Causqua Creeks most of the way to the meadows. Some sections are very muddy, but they usually improve as the summer wears on. Just before reaching the meadows, the trail drops down slightly and crosses a small tributary to Causqua Creek. It then follows the draw up to a complex watershed at the head of Gramaphone, Causqua, Reiseter and Harold Price Creeks.

Beyond that, the trail bears slightly to the right and cuts across the headwaters of the most westerly fork of Reiseter Creek, then it reverts more or less to the previous heading and starts to drop gently as it crosses over into the Harold Price watershed. After skirting a large meadow at the 1350 m level, the trail follows a tributary to Harold Price Creek down into the Basin at elevation 1200 m. It is an extensive, open area, mostly marshy and covered with scrub willow, with Harold Price Creek meandering through, heading north. From above, it is a very attractive setting, but the soggy ground and willow bushes makes it tough country to hike through.

Once the trail breaks out into the upper level meadows, it becomes very sketchy where the ground is wet, but with care, it can be followed all the way down into Harold Price Basin. After leaving the last meadow, there are many windfalls across the trail on the way down through the timber.

To reach the upper level meadows, allow 2-3 hours from the end of the logging road and slightly less on the way back.

DIRECTIONS:
Access to the trail is by a logging road off Telkwa High Road 10 km east of Moricetown. From Smithers, travel west on Hwy.16 about 34 km to Moricetown. Turn right on Telkwa High Road and follow it back in the direction of Smithers for 10 km. Immediately after crossing Meed Creek, the

Looking west over Causqua Creek headwaters
towards Rocher Deboule Range.

Headwaters of Harold Price Creek;
cabin is on the semi-open ridge, to the far left.

logging road continues straight ahead where Telkwa High Road bears right up a hill. An alternative approach is to travel east from Smithers on Hwy.16 and access Telkwa High Road via Babine Lake Road and Snake Road. Turn left onto Telkwa High Road and follow it west towards Moricetown for about 12 km before turning right onto the logging road at Meed Creek.

The logging road drops down slightly and crosses Meed Creek less than a kilometer from the start. For the next kilometer it is level, then it climbs up a couple of switchbacks. Shortly thereafter, at km 3, where it forks, take the left branch (#2200) that heads downhill again. At about km 5, cross Grama-phone Creek and at the fork just beyond km 6, take the right branch that starts climbing right away. The elevation at the fork is about 600 m and from there the road goes up over a distance of 6 km to 1050 m, where it splits into three. To that point the road is good and passable for standard vehicles. At the split, take the middle road, which is rough and muddy. It goes on for another kilometer, gaining 50 m or so in elevation. With 4-wheel drive it is just passable towards the end of summer when it has dried up.

Beyond the centre of the cut-block, the road becomes impassable. In any case, nothing is gained by following it farther. To find the trail, head almost due north, straight for the far side of the cut-block. A tall, blaze-marked tree shows where to enter the standing timber.

COMMENTS:

This trail is the original access route from Hazelton and Moricetown to the Cronin Mine on the east side of the range. It was cut for pack-horses that were used at the beginning of this century to carry supplies in and high grade ore out. Hazelton, at the head of navigation on the Skeena, was then the major centre of communications and commerce for the region and pack-trails radiated out in all directions. Only after the railway was completed, did other access routes open up to places like the Cronin Mine.

As far as the open meadow area, the trail has been used and maintained over the years by hunting guides to gain access, not only to the meadows, but to the high country a couple of kilometers away to the northeast. With the accelerating pace of logging in the Smithers area, the roads were built that now make that part of the trail much shorter and easier to access.

The great expanse of interconnected meadows and the open country above, makes the area ideal for hiking, horse riding and particularly ski touring. However, in winter, the logging road is at best plowed only part way and the days are short, so the time required to ski in is a problem. Partly for that reason, the Bulkley Valley Cross-Country Ski Club has put a cabin in the upper meadow, making it possible to stay overnight without carrying in full winter camping gear. It is also becoming apparent that with the cabin, access to the Grassy Mountain country, at the north end of Babine Mountains Recreation Area, via Harold Price Basin, could be quite feasible. If that is found to be the case, it opens the way to another exciting area and alternative exit routes, such as Reiseter Creek Trail [BS5].

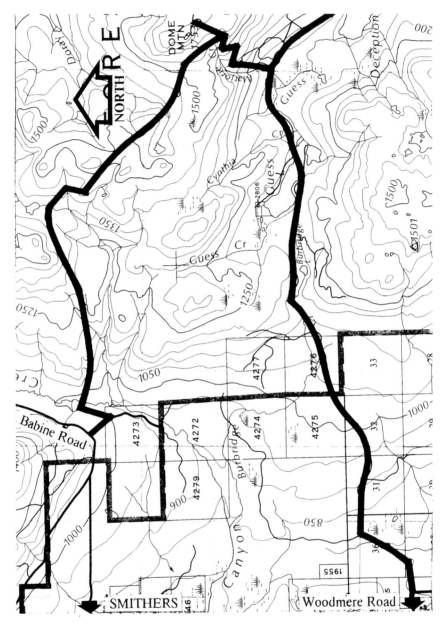

DOME MOUNTAIN ROAD [BS11]

(Part of Map 93L/NE)

1cm=1km, 50m contour interval

DOME MOUNTAIN ROAD [BS11]

LOCATION:
Babine Range (South), near Smithers.

MAPS REQUIRED:
93L/10 Quick (1:50,000)
93L/15 Driftwood Creek (1:50,000)
93L Smithers (1:250,000)

DIRECTIONS:
From Smithers, proceed as for Cronin Creek Road [BS9], but just after the km 20 mark and the high point on Babine Road, turn right onto Dome Mountain Road. After heading southeasterly for about a kilometer, mostly downhill, turn left onto a road going north. A kilometer or so farther along, it turns right to head easterly, crosses Canyon Creek and then climbs steeply for the next 5 km to about 1450 m. The road continues for another 7 km to the base of Dome Mountain, heading generally southeast. It goes up and down a lot through semi-open country, much of it very marshy. Some sections of the road are too muddy to be passable even with 4-wheel drive.

COMMENTS:
It is an easy scramble up the hillside to the 1750 m summit of Dome Mountain, less than a kilometer from the base and only 300 m higher.

Another road approaches the summit from the southwest. It switch-backs up from elevation 1150 m along Marjorie Creek, a tributary to Guess Creek. That road ties into a complex network of logging and mining roads south of Dome Mountain. The road heading west follows the creek upstream to Guess Lake and then passes Burbridge Lake before dropping down gradually to elevation 800 m, some 20 km from Dome Mountain. There it joins Woodmere Road that in turn leaves Hwy.16 a few kilometers east of Telkwa.

A road from the east also provides access to Dome Mountain, but due to mining activities, that road may be closed to the public.

The area is much used by snowmobilers. About half way along Dome Mountain Road, they have a cabin by a chain of small lakes. A couple of kilometers in from Woodmere Road, they usually maintain a connecting trail that starts off along a side road heading north to eventually join Dome Mountain Road near Babine Road. That makes it possible to do a 45-50 km round trip, in by one road, across Dome Mountain and out the other. The same trip can of course be made on skis, or by mountain bike in the summer.

The semi-alpine area surrounding Dome Mountain and the mountain itself provide excellent terrain for skiing. In its isolated location at the south-eastern extremity of the Babine Range, Dome Mountain also offers wonderful views in all directions.

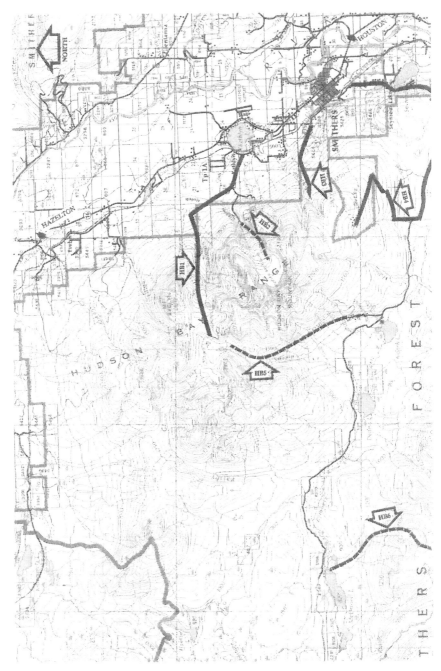

HUDSON BAY RANGE

1cm = 2km , 50m contour interval

HUDSON BAY RANGE

It is unusual to find such perfect harmony as exists between Hudson Bay Mountain and its surroundings. By its size and graceful proportions and with its jagged peaks and dazzling glaciers, it commands attention from any point in the Bulkley Valley. Yet, without the wide valley and open, gently rolling fields to add contrast and perspective, the mountain would be just one of many in a country full of mountains. Not quite perhaps, height might save it from obscurity. At 2560 m, its highest peak is surpassed only by the Seven Sisters among all the mountains visible from Highway 16. From the Bulkley River at its base to the summit, the total vertical relief is over 2000 m.

To experience the full impact of the impressive relief and to see and photograph this lovely mountain, drive along the Telkwa Hi Road instead of the main highway from Telkwa to Moricetown. Early morning or late afternoon on a sunny spring day are the best times. The Hudson Bay Range is in full view across the valley for most of the 50-odd kilometers. Light green trees and fields fill the foreground, the darker green of conifers define the lower slopes and the jagged, snowcapped summits stand out sharply against the deep blue sky. Below the peaks are the shining, white glaciers. The scene is unforgettable and inspiring.

No wonder the Bulkley Valley is one of the favoured areas in West Central British Columbia where people settle and choose to stay and where the quality of life is held in higher regard than material possessions.

Along its main axis from Seymour Lake in the southeast to Trout Creek in the northwest, Hudson Bay Range covers close to 25 km. It is about 15 km across, occupying the space between the Bulkley and Zymoetz Rivers. Access to the range and up to timberline via a variety of roads and trails is good along the whole periphery except from the northwest. In the heyday of exploration and prospecting, according to the 1911 Annual Report of the Minister of Mines, there was also access from that direction by way of trails that linked Trout and Passby Creeks. Some trail clearing now in progress should soon make direct access to that area possible once again.

GEOGRAPHICAL FEATURES

A thick series of sedimentary and volcanic rocks (Hazelton Group) form most of the mountains in the Hazelton and Smithers areas. The Hudson Bay Range is no exception. These rocks are invaded by numerous granodiorite stocks (Bulkley intrusions) that may be related to the batholithic rocks of the Coast Mountains 50 km or so to the west. These intrusions are of considerable significance, since mineral deposits are likely to be found in or closely associted with them (19). Those with a particular interest in the geology of the area should make a point of referring to Gottesfeld's book (1) on that subject.

The four major peaks of of Hudson Bay Mountain are located on a well defined summit ridge more than 3 km long. Lateral ridges extend out at right angles to the spine. The two most prominent projections towards the northeast embrace the largest and most visible glacier. Another major glacier, less visible because of its orientation, lies just to the north, at the head of Toboggan Creek. The range has no other significant glaciers.

At the northwest end of the main summit ridge, a low pass (1650 m) at the head of Silvern and Toboggan Creeks separates the range into two sections. The northwest section is lower and less precipitous than the section southeast of the pass and is again split by a 1500 m pass between the heads of Silvern and Passby Creeks. In the Y-shaped area containing the headwaters of Toboggan, Silvern and Passby Creeks, the terrain is rolling and almost park-like. There are several small lakes and extensive marsh and meadow areas within this basin. Other than that, the range has few high elevation lakes, but all around the base there are many fine lakes.

The rocks above and to the east of Lower Silvern Lake are rich in fossils (Middle Jurassic). Many interesting specimens are easily accessible in the scree slopes below.

In general, timberline is at around 1500 m. Below, the slopes are well covered with spruce, balsam, poplar and jackpine. The timber is mostly thick and the undergrowth heavy, particularly on the lower slopes. Travelling through the bush where there are no cleared roads or trails is, more often than not, frustratingly slow and unpleasant.

Hudson Bay Range is no longer prime habitat for any of the large mammals. The area it covers is relatively small and is isolated from other ranges by fairly distinct natural and man-made barriers. Easy access and the intense mining and mineral exploration activities that have taken place throughout the range for the best part of the last century have certainly had an impact. Caribou no longer inhabit the range. Grizzly bears, wolves and mountain goats are rare. Moose, deer, black bears and coyote are still present, perhaps in greater number than ever before. Wolverine, lynx and smaller furbearing animals are around, but are very shy and rarely seen, squirrels being an exception. Above timberline, marmots and lemmings can be seen in fluctuating numbers. Porcupines, being placid, not easily disturbed and not subject to hunting pressure by man or beast, seem to thrive. Birds of all kinds, representative of the latitude and climatic conditions, can always be seen.

MINING

Mineral deposits containing one or more of the following metals are present: gold, silver, lead, zinc, copper, bismuth and molybdenum. These deposits occur predominantly in four localities: at the head of Toboggan Creek, at Glacier Gulch, at Simpson Creek and on the slopes above Aldrich Lake. Coal deposits also occur in the vicinity of Glacier Gulch.

Silver-lead-zinc ore (galena) was first discovered in 1905 near the present Duthie (Sil-Van) mine. During the next few years, intense prospecting quickly disclosed most of the other significant ore bodies (19). An exception was the body of molybdenum ore underneath the ice of the main glacier. The presence of an underlying intrusive stock was indicated by boulders of porphyritic granodiorite found near the foot of the glacier in Glacier Gulch. Several small veinlets of molybdenite were also known to exist near the foot of the glacier. However, it was not until the 1960s, when interest in molybdenum picked up and Climax Molydenum entered the picture, that drilling through the ice, and later from tunnel headings under the ice, disclosed a significant ore body.

Between 1910 and 1930, development work was carried out intermittently and small shipments of high grade ore were made from various properties. Duthie Mine came into operation with underground work starting in 1922. For the next five years, occasional shipments of hand-sorted silver-lead-zinc ore were made. In 1927 a 50 tons/day mill was installed and operated until 1930. From then until 1940 there was very little activity, but in 1940 and 1941 the mine operated again on a small scale. In 1946 and 1947 there was further work and in the 1950s, after continued exploration by Sil-Van, that company eventually installed and operated a 150 tons/day mill for a few years (19). Off and on over the years since, the mine has been active to varying degrees, but it has always remained a small scale operation.

Except for the Ski Hill Road, which is of relatively recent origin, it is the extensive mining and exploration activity that took place during the first half of this century that accounts for the easy access to Hudson Bay Range from nearly all directions.

HISTORICAL NOTES

Smithers (22), the community that is now so intimately associated with Hudson Bay Mountain, and the major centre in the Bulkley Valley, is not in fact among the original communities of the area. It was born of the railway and first saw the light of day in 1913. Telkwa, already an established community, would have been the location chosen for the railway divisional point but for the fact that it was on the wrong side of the Bulkley River. Technically, Hubert, a small community a few kilometers east of Telkwa, was the obvious choice. The only problem was that it was too obvious and land speculation, that inevitably seems to have accompanied railway construction, had driven the price of land beyond what Grand Trunk Pacific was prepared to pay. In great secrecy, the location finally selected was a straight section of track 20 km west of Telkwa. It was named Smithers after the chairman of Grand Trunk Pacific. As a scenic location, the new divisional point could not have been chosen better, but for construction purposes, the choice was a nightmare since it was in the middle of a great swamp! Lovely Lake Kathlyn nearby, went by the unromantic name of Chicken Lake in those days.

The Bulkley Valley remained unsettled longer than most other parts of southern and central British Columbia even though there was considerable activity on the periphery. The Telegraph Trail from the Cariboo that followed the Bulkley River en route to Hazelton and points north, was pushed through in 1866, but the adjacent country remained virtually unexplored.

From 1890 to 1892, the provincial government made preliminary surveys of the area at the same time as the wagon road from Hazelton to Moricetown was laid out.

In 1898 Hudson's Bay Company initiated farming in the Bulkley Valley by establishing a ranch on the Telegraph Trail at Driftwood Creek to winter pack horses and grow hay and vegetables. The ranch, looking out across the valley towards the mountain beyond, gave the name Hudson Bay to that mountain. As a result of favourable reports from the Company about the agricultural potential of the Bulkley Valley and because of subsequent promotion of the area by the government and land speculators, settlers began to trickle in.

The first real settlement began in about 1903 along the shores of what was then known as Aldermere Lake and now variously as MacLure or Tyhee Lake. Here the little village of Aldermere was established in 1904 and flourished as the commercial and cultural centre of the Bulkley Valley until 1914 when the railway came and other centres grew up and replaced it. In fact, as early as 1907, the rival community of Telkwa sprang up where the Telegraph Trail swung down to the banks of the Bulkley, across from the mouth of the Telkwa River.

In 1908 and 1909, the trail from Hazelton to Aldermere was upgraded to a waggon road with a bridge across the Bulkley constucted at Moricetown (15,23).

Since those days, the Bulkley Valley has flourished in a quiet way and has become the most important agricultural, beef and dairy production area in West Central British Columbia. Mining has remained one of the cornerstones of the local economy. Over the years the woods industry has become an important element of the economy, as has government services and the service industry in general. Fortunately, no one industry or activity has grown to the point of becoming dominant. The economic base has therefore remained broad and varied with the result that steady but unspectacular growth has been the norm, rather than the boom and bust cycles so characteristic of many other northern communities. The majority of people in the area have developed deep roots and the pride in and love for the community that is so essential to the quality of life.

FUTURE PROSPECTS

The ski development on Hudson Bay Mountain has put the area well on the way to becoming a major centre for winter recreation. Recognition of the potential for cross-country skiing and ski touring in the winter and for back-packing and hiking in the summer is slowly emerging. There is no question that the area will eventually become a choice destination for the growing number of tourists who are interested in exploring the back-country whether it be on foot, on skis, on horseback or by snowmobile. The road-

Hudson Bay Mountain; alpine ski area on extreme left.

bound tourists will probably keep coming, but their contribution to the local economy will decline in importance relative to that of the visitors who come to base themselves in the area for a week or two. The back-country that cradles the Bulkley Valley is in all probability the last major "gold mine" around that is still largely unknown. To make that "mine" work for the community, first its potential needs to be recognized locally, then the needs of potential visitors, initially for good information, have to be understood and satisfied. A prerequisite to that would be some research to determine how and where to reach them.

Tourism must eventually become another cornerstone of the economic base in the Bulkley Valley, as in other parts of the Province. Many other resources are being depleted at an alarming rate. To maintain a broadly based, varied economy, a greater emphasis on tourism is rapidly becoming a necessity rather than a matter of choice.

A tourist industry depends, as do many other economic activities and all outdoor recreation, on a shared resource base. That is now well understood, but is accepted only reluctantly, if at all, when resource management decisions are made. Our system of government is poorly structured to deal with that problem. Fortunately there are encouraging signs that the pressure exerted by public opinion is leading to more thoughtful decisions. Progress in that direction cannot come too quickly for the tourist industry, but it is equally important that the industry itself not be driven by greed or ignorance to over-exploitation. The back-country can only accommodate limited human intrusion without loosing its appeal.

The harmony between Hudson Bay Mountain and the valley it presides over should remain close and even grow with its importance as a prime recreational resource. As always, it will be beautiful to behold and a source of inspiration.

155

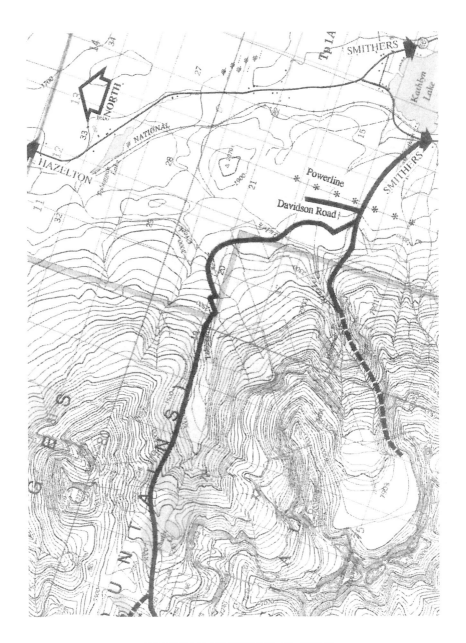

TOBOGGAN CREEK ROAD [HB1]
GLACIER GULCH TRAIL [HB2]
(Part of Map 93L/14)
1cm=2/3km, 100ft.(30m) contour interval

TOBOGGAN CREEK ROAD [HB1]

LOCATION:
Hudson Bay Range, near Smithers.

MAPS REQUIRED:
93L/14 Smithers (1:50,000)
93L Smithers (1:250,000)

DIRECTIONS:
From Smithers, proceed as for Glacier Gulch Trail [HB2], but after following Glacier Gulch Road for 2 km, turn right onto a side road just beyond Davidson Road. The road is rough and somewhat overgrown, but remains more or less level as it follows the base of the mountain in a northwesterly direction. After 2 km there is a bridge across Glacier Gulch and in another 2 km, the road crosses Toboggan Creek. If the bridge is intact, it may be possiible to continue up the hill on the other side for a kilometer or so with a standard vehicle, but beyond that the road becomes too steep and rough. From the Toboggan Creek bridge at elevation 600 m, the road continues on for 9 or 10 km to near the 2000 m level on the northwest ridge of Hudson Bay Mountain, above Schufer Lake. With a 4-wheel drive vehicle, it may be passable to elevation 1500 m, 7 km from the bridge. At that point, close to the pass over into the Silvern Creek drainage, it is often blocked by snow until late in the summer. Even when it is not, the continuation of the road is so rough that it is virtually impassable.

COMMENTS:
The first part of the climb up the road is through heavy timber and nothing much can be seen, but then the view across Toboggan Creek opens up and becomes very impressive, with Toboggan Glacier as a centrepiece. Looking back, the Bulkley Valley also comes into view.

Toboggan Creek Road is by far the most spectacular access route to Hudson Bay Mountain. It is also very direct and straightforward, but for that reason, it is uncomfortably steep in places. The summit ridge is easily reached from the end of the road, but is no place for other than suitably equipped and experienced mountaineers. Above the 2300 m level, the ridge narrows to a knife edge, there are several gendarmes along it and the exposure is severe on both sides. However, the wide part of the ridge, just beyond the end of the road, is interesting and the views in all directions are very spectacular.

From the 1500 m level on the road, there is a trail leading through the pass and down to Upper Silvern Lake. It skirts the east shore of the lake, continues on to the lower lake and angles up the slope on the east side, where it joins Silvern Lakes Trail [HB5] coming up from the other side of Hudson Bay Mountain. Crossing over the mountain via this route is a very pleasant,

Toboggan Glacier.

but long one day hike. It is best done in the reverse direction, up Silvern Lakes Trail and down Toboggan Creek Road.

Silvern Lakes basin and the outposts of Hudson Bay Range north and west of the lakes, is a wonderful area for hiking, camping and skiing. An added attraction is the fish in Silvern Lakes, even though they are very small. The talus slopes east of the lower lake are rich in fossils.

The whole range has been extensively explored for minerals over the years going right back to the beginning of this century. At the head of Toboggan Creek, the oldest claims, the Silver Creek group at elevation 1700 m above Schufer Lake, were staked originally by P. Schufer in 1908. It was to continue the development of those claims that the trail up Toboggan Creek was upgraded to a tractor road in 1938 by the Public Works Department. It has since been improved and maintained from time to time by various exploration and mining companies.

GLACIER GULCH TRAIL [HB2]
(Route map on p.156)

LOCATION:
Hudson Bay Range, near Smithers.

MAPS REQUIRED:
93L/14 Smithers (1:50,000)
93L Smithers (1:250,000)

ROUTE DESCRIPTION:
Just over 2 km from start of trail at elevation 750 m to edge of glacier at about 1750 m, where it ends.

The trail starts from the parking area and remains on the true right side of Glacier Gulch as it climbs steeply through timber at first and then across open sidehills. In the timber it is a good, well maintained trail, but out on the open scree slopes, some sections have been almost obliterated by small slides. Numerous sketchy tracks exist where people have taken different routes to link up sections of trail. It is not a problem to find a route up even if the trail is lost, but the footing is much better on than off the trail. At the top, the trail gradually peters out as it comes alongside the snout of the glacier.

Allow 2-3 hours up to the glacier and 1-2 hours down.

DIRECTIONS:
Going west on Highway 16 from Smithers, turn left onto Lake Kathlyn Road after about 4 km. Just before the turnoff and at other points on the way, there are signposts indicating "Glacier Gulch and Twin Falls". Follow the signposts, cross the railway track and then turn left onto Glacier Gulch Road. At that point there is a signpost indicating 4 km to Twin Falls Recreation Site. On the way, close to a kilometer up the hill after passing Davidson Road on the right, a branch road goes off to the left. It switchbacks up to an adit used many years ago for exploratory drilling under the glacier. There is no access to the glacier that way, but the road does provide some fine views of the Bulkley Valley.

Continue on beyond the parking area of Twin Falls Recreation Site and look for the sign indicating the start of Glacier Gulch Trail on the left.

COMMENTS:
Twin Falls is well worth a visit even for those who have no intention of going on up the trail to the glacier. The waterfalls created where the twin creeks that issue from the glacier tumble several hundred meters down into the gulch, are very spectacular, particularly in early summer when the snow-melt is at its peak. Apart from the scenery, there are some visible remains of previous mining activity, mostly for coal.

In addition to parking and picnic facilities and the main Glacier Gulch

Trail, there is also a well constructed trail along the bank of the creek, so it is easy to get quite close to the falls. Much of the site was badly damaged by a large slide that occurred during the winter of 1989, but the facilities have since been restored. On the plus side, with most of the vegetation along the

creek below the falls wiped out by the slide, it is considerably easier than before to photograph the falls. Even so, photography is tricky because of the confined space and problems with lighting.

Those who go up the trail will enjoy spectacular views looking out over the Bulkley Valley. Once the vegetation is left behind and the trail moves out onto the open scree slopes, it is unsafe for inexperienced hikers and children who are not kept under close control. The footing is insecure and the exposure considerable. There is a significant risk of rocks, snow and ice crashing down from the slopes above and only in a few places is it safe to linger. Towards the top of the trail, there is a good view of the glacier with the towering peaks of Hudson Bay Mountain in the background.

In some ways the glacier is less impressive at close range, particularly late in the summer when the snow cover has all gone and the ice is seen to be rather dirty and laden with debris - mostly natural, but also some garbage left behind by mineral exploration. Extensive drilling has taken place, initially through the ice, to probe the rock below. The later stages of exploratory drilling took place from tunnels in the rock below the ice. It appears that a large body of molybdenum ore exists underneath the glacier.

It is easy to get onto the ice from the end of the trail. As the underlying rock is relatively smooth and only slopes moderately, the glacier is not heavily crevassed except near the edges, where the slope is more severe. That does not mean it is completely safe to move around on the ice without the proper equipment and experience, only that the crevasses do not impede progress to any great extent.

There are no obvious or easy routes off the glacier other than back along the trail, however, there are several possible routes onto adjacent ridges for experienced climbers.

Glacier Gulch Trail goes up on the left side of cirque.

SIMPSON CREEK ROAD [HB3]

LOCATION:
Hudson Bay Range, near Smithers.

MAPS REQUIRED:
93L/14 Smithers (1:50,000)
93L Smithers (1:250,000)

DIRECTIONS:
   In Smithers, follow Railway Avenue north and continue over the level crossing onto Zobnick Road heading straight towards the base of the mountain. Half a kilometer beyond the railway crossing, keep straight ahead onto a side road, which is the beginning of Simpson Creek Road, instead of following the main road as it turns right. Shortly thereafter, the road passes under a powerline and bears right as it starts to climb up the hillside on a northwesterly heading. The general direction remains much the same for the first kilometer, but the road then switches to a southerly heading for the next kilometer. At that point, near elevation 800 m, the road levels out and heads northwesterly again. Avoid the side road that continues up to the left and crosses Chicken Creek almost right away.
   The level section of road is less than a kilometer, then it climbs steeply for 3-4 km, heading westerly, straight for the basin at the head of the south fork of Simpson Creek, where the road ends near the 1500 m level. A kilometer or so before the road ends, a branch goes left to the old Snowshoe group of mineral claims in a clearing a short distance away. The clearing, just below timberline on the ridge that cuts off the view into Simpson Basin, is visible from town.

COMMENTS:
   Like so much of the Hudson Bay Range, the basin at the head of Simpson Creek has seen intensive mineral exploration and some small scale mining over the years. The Empire group of claims, covering much of the basin, was first staked in 1908 by Simpson. Some remains of all the activity can still be found.
   To the north, on the spur between the two forks of Simpson Creek, was the Jessie group of claims. A trail heads off to the right just before the end of the road and goes first to what remains of the associated cabin and then to the mine. Higher up on the north fork of Simpson Creek were the Heather and Yukon groups of claims.
   In part, the road is in poor condition. With a standard vehicle it is not passable beyond the powerline crossing. At times, some 4-wheel drive vehicles may get about half way up the road. A mountain bike certainly speeds up the descent, but it is questionable if that justifies the effort of pushing it up.

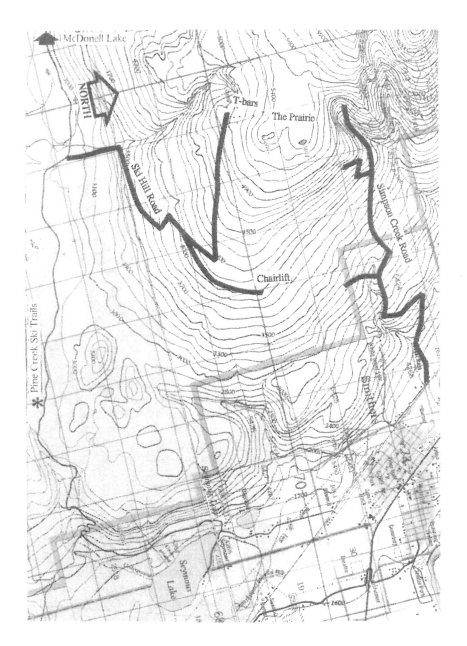

SIMPSON CREEK ROAD [HB3]
SKI HILL ROAD [HB4]
(Part of Map 93L/14)
1cm=2/3km, 100ft.(30m) contour interval

162

Bulkley Valley and Babine Mountains from Simpson Creek Road.

From the top of the road, the view looking out over the Bulkey Valley, with the Babine Range as a backdrop, is very impresssive, but on the way up, the road is in the timber and there is not much to be seen. Considering also that the same view can had with far less effort by a drive up the Ski Area Road [HB4], on the other side of the mountain, followed by an easy hike up and across the ridge, Simpson Creek Road can hardly be recommended just for the view.

The road is of some interest to skiers as a direct route from the mountain right down into Smithers. It is essential to know the area well and also be a good skier to get down safely that way. The first problem is to find the top of the road while avoiding both the steep drop into Simpson basin to the left and the sheer rock face less than a kilometer to the right. In between, the drop down through the bush to the Snowshoe claims branch road is not overly steep. Skiing down the road could be another problem unless snow conditions are good.

SKI HILL ROAD [HB4]
(Route map on p.162)

LOCATION:
Hudson Bay Range, near Smithers.

MAPS REQUIRED:
93L/14 Smithers (1:50,000)
93L Smithers (1:250,000)

DIRECTIONS:
In Smithers, turn off Hwy.16 at "Ski Area" sign, follow King Street down to Railway Avenue and turn left. In about 2 km, the road turns sharp right and crosses the railway. Less than a kilometer after that, turn sharp left at another "Ski Area" sign. A kilometer from there, at Seymour Lake fork, bear right, following the "Ski Area" signpost. There the road starts to climb as it works its way up and around the southeast ridge of Hudson Bay Mountain.

Some 10 km from Smithers, near elevation 900 m, is the parking lot for Pine Creek cross-country ski area. The road is fairly level for the next 5 km to the fork, where the Ski Hill Road is the branch straight ahead. Over the next 6 km, the road climbs steadily all the way to elevation 1500 m, where it ends at the base of Ski Smithers' Hudson Bay Mountain alpine skiing area.

COMMENTS:
This is a good gravel road, well maintained and open all year round. The ski area offers good lift facilities and runs on both sides of the ridge. Snow conditions are normally great for downhill skiing from December to April and at the top of the runs there are wonderful views in all directions. The area is also excellent for cross-country ski touring with terrain to suit most snow and weather conditions.

It is sometimes possible to ski all the way up the southeast ridge to the 2500 m south summit of Hudson Bay Mountain, but often it is so wind blown higher up that skiing is not very pleasant. Hiking up to the south summit in the summer is not difficult and the view from the top makes the effort worthwhile. Straight down, 500 m below, is the glacier that faces the highway and is such a prominent feature of Hudson Bay Mountain. The first recorded ascent of the central peak by Shives, Woodsworth, Dahlie and Culbert in 1962 was via the south summit and the connecting ridge. It is almost a knife ridge and should be attempted only by experienced mountaineers.

At the 1650 m level on the southeast ridge is an extensive area that is known locally as the "Prairie" because it is so flat. By crossing over the "Prairie" from the downhill ski area, it is possible to reach the top of Simpson Creek Road [HB3] and go down that way. Considerable care is required to avoid the steep drop into Simpson basin on the left and at the same time the sheer rock face on the right. In between it is fairly easy to reach the road.

SILVERN LAKES TRAIL [HB5]

LOCATION:
Hudson Bay Range, near Smithers.

MAPS REQUIRED:
93L/14 Smithers (1:50,000)
93L Smithers (1:250,000)

ROUTE DESCRIPTION:
From start of trail, where McDonell Lake road crosses Henderson Creek, to Lower Silvern Lake, it is about 9 km. In that distance, the trail climbs steadily on an easy grade from 900 m to nearly 1500 m at the lake.

The first part of the trail is actually an old skid road that more or less follows the true left bank of the creek up and joins a mining road shortly after passing some old cabins. Turn left and follow that road, which continues on for about a kilometer to what remains of the workings and cabins of the Victory group of claims. To find where the trail starts, stay on the road until, after a sharp right turn, it bears left to head straight up the slope. At that point, some of the mine workings are clearly visible. Where the road turns right and heads over to some old cabins, make a left turn and follow the hillside around to a tailings pile. The trail can be picked up quite easily near the base of the pile, on the far side. Initially the trail is level, but soon it starts to climb gently. It is well defined and in fair condition except for some windfalls higher up.

The trail eventually works its way around to the west side of Hudson Bay Mountain and up to timberline. Before that, it emerges briefly into the open where it drops down a hundred meters or so to cross the Red Valley, so called because in some lighting conditions, the rocks have a striking red colour. At several points along the trail farther ahead, the same colour is evident in the mud.

Once across Red Valley, the trail climbs steeply to cross a final, small ridge before it heads into Silvern Lakes basin.

Allow a good 3-4 hours hiking to reach the first lake and maybe an hour less to return.

DIRECTIONS:
From Smithers, proceed as for the Ski Hill Road [HB4], but at the fork 5 km beyond Pine Creek parking area, keep left on the road signed "Copper River Guest Ranch 24 km". The fork is also km 0 of McDonell Lake Forest Road.

Just before km 6, keep left at the fork. The road to the right goes to Duthie Mine. It is also possible to go in that way to reach the trail because the road to the Victory claims starts at Duthie Mine. However, by continuing

Silvern Lakes Basin with the upper lake.

on the main road to km 8, the walking distance is slightly less. Just before the bridge across Henderson Creek, there is a gravel pit, which is a convenient place to park. The skid road starts right behind the pit.

COMMENTS:

This is an easy route to Silvern Lake and what is by far the most attractive area within the range for hiking, camping and ski touring. The wide open basin is like a park with gently sloping meadows and small clumps of trees. At the height of the alpine flower season in August, the whole area is a riot of colour. Silvern Lakes are full of fish, very small, but tasty enough for all that. The scree slopes east of the lower lake are rich in fossils.

From the lower lake, there is a continuation of the trail to the upper lake, along its east shore and then up to the pass where it joins Toboggan Creek Road [HB1]. That connection makes it possible to cross right over the range. The trip can be made in a long day. If it is done on skis, keep in mind that Toboggan Creek Road is very steep. Skiing down the road is for experts only, unless snow conditions are just perfect.

At the Victory claims, there is another trail going off in the opposite direction to Silvern Lakes Trail. From the old cabins, it climbs gently in a southerly direction after crossing a small creek. At about the 1200 m level, it intersects a mining road that switchbacks directly up from Duthie Mine. By following that road to the top, it is possible to cut across to the end of the Ski Hill Road [HB4], a few kilometers farther east. It is mostly open hillside, but cut by some deep gullies that have to be crossed.

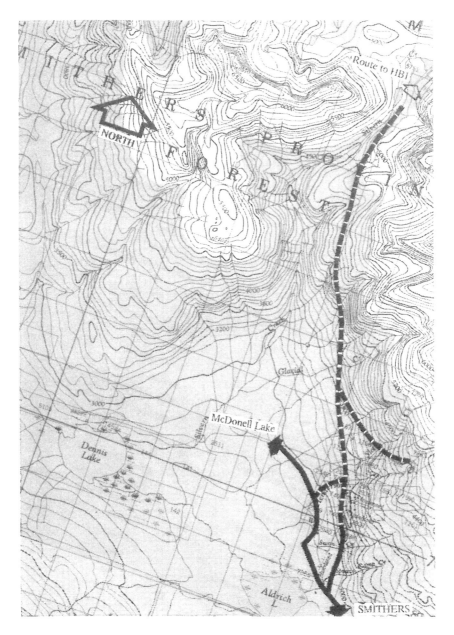

SILVERN LAKES TRAIL [HB5]

(Part of Map 93L/14)
1cm=2/3km, 100ft.(30m) contour interval

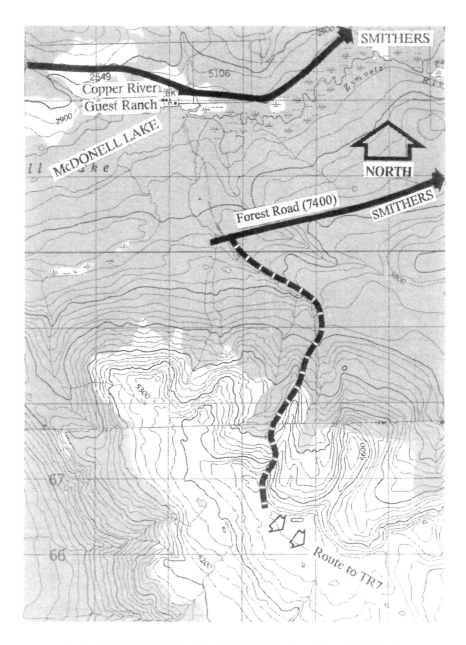

McDONELL LAKE TRAIL [HB6]

(Part of Maps 93L/12&13)
1cm=1/2km, 100ft.(30m) contour interval

McDONELL LAKE TRAIL [HB6]

LOCATION:
McDonell Lake, near Smithers.

MAPS REQUIRED:
93L/12 Milk Creek (1:50,000)
93L/13 McDonell Lake (1:50,000)
93L Smithers (1:250,000)

ROUTE DESCRIPTION:
The trail starts at km 9 of Forest Service road 7400, near the east end of McDonell Lake.   Over a distance of close to 6 km, it climbs from elevation 900 m at the road to 1750 m on the crest of the ridge south of the lake. It is a well defined trail in good condition.

The trail climbs quite slowly along the true right bank of an un-named creek to 1200 m at about the half way point. There it crosses to the other side
of the creek and climbs steeply away from it up towards the crest of a lateral ridge. It crosses the ridge close to timberline, but then drops part way down into the valley on the other side and follows it up to the small basin at the head of the middle fork of the un-named creek. The trail reaches timberline in the basin at about 1500 m, continues through the basin and up the east headwall, back on to the lateral ridge, and follows it up to the main ridge.
Allow a good 3 hours to timberline and about 2 hours down.

DIRECTIONS:
From Smithers, proceed as for Ski Hill Road [HB4], but at the fork 5 km beyond Pine Creek parking area, turn left onto the road signed "Copper River Guest Ranch 24 km". That point is km 0 of McDonell Lake Forest Road (7000).At about km 14 (7014),turn left onto McDonell South Forest Road (7300). Just beyond the 7301 marker, turn right onto the 7400 road. Near the 7409 marker and just before a bridge, look for the signed trail head at the top of a steep bank on the left.

COMMENTS:

McDonell Lake Trail leads to ridge on the right.

From the top end of the trail, heading southeasterly, there is a connecting route via the main ridge system to Winfield Creek Road [TR7]. That road extends as a "cat" track up to and then along the ridge. The terrain is well suited for hiking and also for skiing and horse riding.

The ridge is well located to command exceptionally fine views in all directions. Particularly impressive is the view of the Howson Range to the southwest.

TELKWA RANGE

This is a somewhat ill defined, sprawling range, not distinguished by any really significant peaks. Topographically, if not geologically, it could well be described as an appendage to the Coast Range, projecting easterly some 60 km to the confluence of the Bulkley and Morice Rivers. In the west, it is separated from the Coast Range by a depression where the Telkwa and Burnie Rivers originate. The northern boundary is in reality the Telkwa River, but here it is most convenient to include the area to the north as far as the Zymoetz River. To the south and east, the Morice and Bulkley Rivers mark the boundaries. From north to south, the area covers approximately 80 km.

Access to the range is not particularly good in spite of the fact that, except on the west side, there are logging roads all around the periphery and up the Telkwa River. The latter does provide limited access to alpine areas on both sides of the river, mostly via old mining roads. One such road going up Howson Creek penetrates right to the centre of the range, but the key bridge across the Telkwa River was washed out many years ago, so the road is difficult to reach. At low water and when the river is frozen over, it is not a problem to get across, but those conditions are not always predictable.

Just upstream of where the bridge across to Howson Creek road used to be, a mining road provides access to much of the alpine country on the ridge north of Telkwa River. That road is generally kept in reasonable condition because it is also used for access to two microwave stations, one operated by B.C. Tel and the other by B.C. Hydro. At one time there was also access from both the north and the south to the more mountainous area west of Sinclair and Serb Creeks. A continuation of the road to McDonell Lake crossed the Zymoetz River and headed south towards claims in the vicinity of Serb Creek, but unfortunately there is no longer a bridge across the Zymoetz. From the south, an old mining trail followed the true left bank of Milk Creek to claims at timberline. That trail is now badly overgrown and very difficult to follow. The start of the trail has been obliterated by B.C. Hydro's powerline right-of-way.

The east end of the range, due south of Telkwa, is the most accessible part. There is an old mining road into Hunter Basin and a couple of other reasonable routes nearby.

GEOGRAPHICAL FEATURES

In a 1907 report (24), W.W. Leach subdivides the rocks in the Telkwa Range into four main groups that in ascending order are: crystalline rocks related to the Coast Range, a porphyrite group, coal-bearing sedimentary rocks and an eruptive group of more recent origin. The porphyrite group occupies by far the greatest area and consists of a great series of of volcanics. These and the overlying, coal-bearing beds have been cut by a series of eruptives that had a marked influence on ore deposition, as they apparently afforded

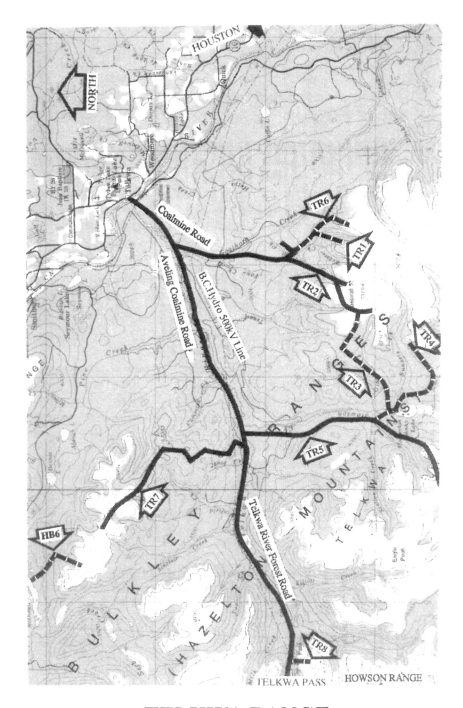

TELKWA RANGE

1cm=3.3km, 500ft.(150m) contour interval

172

channels for the ascent of mineral bearing solutions. In general, no important mineral discoveries have been made except in the immediate vicinity of the eruptives and associated dykes.

South of the Telkwa River, the range is deeply bisected from north to south by a 1000 m pass occupied by Mooseskin Johnny Lake. The outflow is north into Howson Creek. Immediately south of the lake, Thautil River starts and flows south into the Morice River. There is a corresponding cut on the north side of Telkwa River, occupied by Sinclair and Serb Creeks, but it is offset to the west by about 10 km.

The highest peak is a 2340 m unnamed summit a few kilometers east of Mooseskin Johnny Lake. At Telkwa the elevation is about 500 m, so the maximum relief is only just over 1800 m. Even so, the Telkwa Range is an impessive and beautiful sight when viewed from both Smithers and Telkwa. It is particularly pleasing on approaching the Bulkley Valley from the east, when it is the first sight of real mountains after a long drive across the relatively featureless Nechako Plateau.

Everywhere in the range, the glaciers are in retreat. Most of those remaining are small and confined to the north slopes of the highest ridges. Many of the basins dammed by terminal moraines, left by the retreating glaciers, contain small alpine lakes.

While the peaks of the Telkwa Range are quite modest, the Howson Range, directly to the west, has peaks of nearly 2800 m that rank among the highest and most rugged in the whole of West Central British Columbia. They dominate the western skyline and provide some exciting views from many vantage points in the Telkwa Range. It is not too surprising that the Howson Range is one of the few areas in this part of the Province to have attracted the attention of serious mountaineers. The first recorded (25) attempt to climb Howson Peak was made in 1957 by a Canadian Alpine Club party led by Rex Gibson, who was president of the club at the time. The party flew in to Burnie Lake and packed their gear to a base camp established at Sandpiper Lake. Tragedy overtook them on the way up a steep snow gully. There was a slip that resulted in a fall. Several climbers were injured and Rex Gibson subsequently died from his injuries. The following year, another party led by A. Bitterlich succeeded in another attempt to reach the summit after placing a memorial cairn to Gibson on the south col (26).

Above timberline in the Telkwa Range, generally at the 1500 m level, there are large areas where travelling is relatively easy. The terrain is excellent for both hiking and ski touring. At lower elevations, the timber is mainly spruce and balsam mixed with some hemlock and jackpine. In areas that have been logged or burnt, the original forest has been replaced by poplar and jackpine stands. Thick undergrowth and windfalls make it hard to get around in the valley bottoms and on the lower slopes without trails or roads.

While there has been human activity in some parts of the range since the beginning of the century, it is a large area and much of it was seldom visited. For most species of animals, the habitat, has remained relatively undisturbed. Caribou are probably an exception. They still inhabit the range, but apparently in smaller numbers than before. Goats are most likely as plentiful as they have ever been. Much of the range does not suit their requirements and they are found only in the most rugged areas where they have lots of good escape routes. Moose, deer and bears may be seen quite frequently. Furbearing animals, from wolverines down in size to the marten and weasel leave many tracks, but are not often seen since they are quite shy. There are enough of them to support some trapping. Marmots are often seen and heard above timberline.

MINING

The geological features of the Telkwa Range has resulted in some well mineralized areas. Geographically, it is in close proximity to Telkwa, one of the earliest settlements in the Bulkley Valley. That combination of circumstances has brought the area a great deal of attention from prospectors and mining companies, going right back to the beginning of the century. Gold-copper ore was first discovered in 1899 and as early as 1907, a comprehensive report on geological and other features of the Telkwa River and vicinity was produced by W.W. Leach (24).

The coming of the railway spurred interest in coal deposits near Telkwa. Exploratory work, much of it done by Grand Trunk Pacific Railway, disclosed many small coal basins, remnants of a once extensive field. Much of the coal was found to be of high quality, but the formations were broken, flexed and faulted to the extent that mining would be difficult. Even before the railway was completed, work had stopped, since it was considered that not enough coal would be available for railway operation. Oil burning locomotives were then specified for the whole western division, with coal used only on runs east of Prince George.

Coal mining on a small scale to supply local markets did however get underway in 1918 and has continued off and on to this day. A company known as Telkwa Collieries made some shipments to Prince Rupert in the winter of 1917-18 and the coal proved to be satisfactory. By the end of 1918, the rate of production was 30 tons per day and was expected to reach 50. Shipments were transported by horse teams for the first 7 km to Telkwa and then by rail to Prince Rupert. In 1928 and 1929, Telkwa Collieries shipped respectively 1700 and 1500 tons. Production in 1969 was nearly 10,000 tons and the total from the time operations started in 1918 added up to about half a million tons.

Prospecting and exploration for other minerals in the Telkwa Range has been carried on intermittently over the years, but so far has not resulted in any producing mines. Mineralization is mainly confined to several basins associated with the high peaks and ridges. Thus the centres of activity have been Hunter, Hankin and Dominion Basins in the east and Scallon, Howson and Starr Basins towards the west.

All this activity resulted in a considerable network of trails within the

Looking across the Bulkley Valley at the Telkwa Range.

Howson Range from ridge between Telkwa and Zymoetz Rivers.

range, plus two major access routes, one along Goathorn Creek and the other along the Telkwa River and up Howson Creek. Some of the trails are now only of historical interest, but others can still be used to advantage by hikers and skiers. North of the Telkwa River, there are fewer access routes to alpine areas, reflecting the apparently limited extent of mineral exploration in that area. In view of all the prospecting that has been going on for so long in adjacent areas, particularly in the Hudson Bay Range to the north, it is not clear why that should be so.

HISTORICAL NOTES

As a community, Telkwa did not come into being until 1907. However, a short distance away, on the shores of what is now Tyhee Lake, the first small settlement in the Bulkley Valley was established in 1904. It was called Aldermere. The first of the early settlers were then coming into the area and Aldermere became a centre of activity because one of the manned stations on the overland telegraph route to the Yukon was already there.

Not a great deal had been previously known about the Bulkley Valley above Hazelton. The Telegraph Trail passed through there, following the east bank of the river, but beyond that the valley was virgin territory (15,23). There is a reference to the Telkwa River in the 1901 Minister of Mines annual report and in 1903, a prospector named W. Hunter made several important discoveries. The following year a number of prospectors were in the field and made finds that were even better than Hunter's.

At that time, the Bulkley had to be crossed by canoes and horses to reach the Telkwa Range. In his 1907 report (24), Leach mentions that at high water, the crossing was by no means easy. The following year a cable ferry, and some time later, a bridge was put in at a crossing above the point where the Telkwa River joins the Bulkley.

By then, the government had also upgraded the trail between Hazelton and Aldermere to a wagon road and constructed a bridge across the Bulkley at Moricetown Canyon. It was still necessary to travel up the Skeena to Hazelton by river boat, so reaching the Bulkley Valley was an arduous and time consuming business. However, construction of the Grand Trunk Pacific Railway had already started, but whether it would follow the Skeena and Bulkley Rivers all the way or be routed through Telkwa Pass, had not been settled. The latter prospect aroused much interest in the natural resources adjacent to the Telkwa River. Another possible route up the Zymoetz River was also briefly considered. That brought people into the McDonell Lake area.

Eventually, the Bukley-Skeena route was chosen and in 1913, tracks were being laid through the Bulkley Valley. Aldermere was abandoned in favour of Telkwa and Smithers was born as a railway divisional point. In 1914, the last spike was driven near Fraser Lake and the first train through reached Prince Rupert a few days later.

Prospecting activity in the early years of this century led to the creation of a remarkably extensive network of trails, as is evident from a sketch map in the 1911 Minister of Mines annual report. A major trail followed the Zymoetz River and then Limonite Creek up into Telkwa Pass. From there it followed the Telkwa River down to Telkwa. Three access trails to the Telkwa Range are shown, one up Goathorn and Cabinet Creeks into Hunter Basin, one following Tenas Creek up and over the divide to Glacis Creek and down it to Mooseskin Johnny Lake and one up Howson Creek into Howson and Starr Basins. The Howson Creek trail is shown continuing down Thautil River to Morice River. A branch off that trail gave access to Dominion Basin on the south side of the range, opposite Hunter Basin. There was a connecting trail from Hunter Basin to the Tenas-Glacis Creeks trail. Branch trails from Goathorn Creek led to Hankin Basin and the head of Webster Creek, between Hunter and Hankin Basins. For a brief period, while Mooseskin Johnny Lake was a focal point of the trail network, it was the site of several permanent buildings, referred to on some old maps as Howson City!

In 1917, according to the Minister of Mines report for that year, the trail along Howson Creek was upgraded to a wagon road, the cost being split fifty-fifty between the government and the developer. The report for 1925 describes access to Hunter Basin as excellent, by sleigh road for 20 km and then 7 km by trail. Access was further improved that year by a grant from the Department of Mines.

FUTURE PROSPECTS

In common with Babine Mountains Recreation Area, the Telkwa Range is close to Smithers and has some excellent terrain for hiking, ski touring and other outdoor recreation activities. It is somewhat unique in that at Mooseskin Johnny Lake, which is centrally located, there is permanent habitation and cabins for rent. That is also the case at McDonell Lake, on the northern fringe of the area. Such features will almost certainly attract an increasing number of people to the Telkwa Range. There is a good possibility that Howson Creek road will again become accessible if the bridge across the Telkwa River is restored to facilitate logging.

The pace of logging is picking up all around the periphery. Mineral exploration and mining could get underway again quite quickly any time metal or coal prices go up. The potential for resource use conflicts is therefore very real. One such conflict between wildlife and outdoor recreation has been going on for some time. The caribou herd is struggling to make a comeback and there is some concern about the animals being disturbed by snowmobiles and the like. However, as in so many areas, it is the logging versus recreation conflict that is potentially the most serious. The skills and will to resolve such conflicts by reaching viable compromises must come quickly before the timber and recreation resources alike are destroyed.

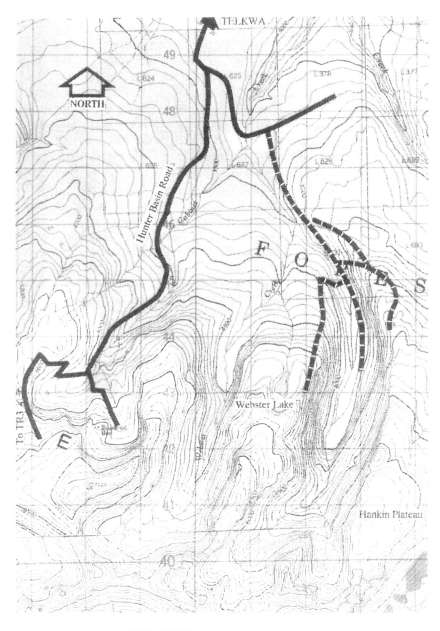

WEBSTER LAKE TRAIL [TR1]
HUNTER BASIN ROAD [TR2]
HANKIN PLATEAU TRAIL [TR6]
(Part of Maps 93L/6&11)
1cm=2/3km, 100ft.(30m) contour interval

178

WEBSTER LAKE TRAIL [TR1]

LOCATION:
Telkwa Range, near Telkwa.

MAPS REQUIRED:
93L/11 Telkwa (1:50,000)
93L Smithers (1:250,000)

ROUTE DESCRIPTION:
For the first 2 km after leaving Goathorn Creek logging road, the route is the same as for Hankin Plateau Trail [TR6], but then it continues along the old mining road for at least another kilometer. At that point, the road emerges from the timber onto an open sidehill above the true right bank of the east fork of Webster Creek. Leave the road there and head straight down the scree slope to the creek. The route is marked, but there is no trail until the creek has been crossed. It is only a sketchy trail, but not unduly difficult to find and follow as it heads more or less straight up the hill west of the creek. After climbing 150 m or so in less than a kilometer, the trail starts to turn left onto a southerly heading. Thereafter, the heading remains much the same for the last 2 km to the end of the trail at elevation 1700 m. It essentially parallels Hankin Plateau Trail, but on the opposite side of the east fork of Webster Creek, where it stays close to the edge of the drop-off to the creek most of the way.

Allow a good 3 hours to reach the 1700 m level from Goathorn Creek logging road and almost as much time to return.

DIRECTIONS:
As for Hankin Plateau Trail [TR6].

COMMENTS:
This short, steep trail is very spectacular, but it is a fairly strenuous hike. The descent from the mining road to the creek is rough and the footing treacherous, particularly if it is wet. Generally the creek is too big to jump over, so unless there is a convenient log bridging it, wading across is the only option.

Along the edge of the drop-off, the trees are small and well spaced out down to elevation 1400 m because so little moisture is retained in the ground. Towards the end, the trail runs along a narrow ridge, high above the east fork of Webster Creek on one side and the deep blue waters of Webster Lake, at the bottom of a crater-like bowl, on the other. Above the lake to the south, the ridge widens to become a mini-plateau that separates the two forks of Webster Creek. Higher up, the plateau narrows again to a ridge that eventually culminates in a 2250 m summit, at the extreme south end.

Webster Lake Trail leads to plateau on the right.

From above timberline, there are fine views in all directions, but even lower down, looking back along the creek or ahead, into and across the basin occupied by the east fork of Webster Creek, is quite impressive. Mountain goats are frequently seen across the basin, just below the edge of Hankin Plateau. The view to the north, out over the Bulkley Valley and the mountains surrounding it, is very attractive and gets better as elevation is gained.

As first seen, quite suddenly from above, at the end of the trail, Webster Lake is like a lovely gem, bright and sparkling, in a dramatic setting. It alone almost makes the effort of hiking up worthwhile.

The mining road at the start continues along on the east side of the valley for a good kilometer beyond the trail turn-off. It ends abruptly for no obvious reason. The open basin at the end of the valley can be reached by dropping down to the creek and picking up a very sketchy trail on the other side. At one time it led to a prospector's camp by the creek higher up.

180

HUNTER BASIN ROAD [TR2]
(Route map on p.178)

LOCATION:
Telkwa Range, near Telkwa.

MAPS REQUIRED:
93L/11 Telkwa (1:50,000)
93L Smithers (1:250,000)

DIRECTIONS:
Turn southwest off Hwy.16 at the traffic lights in Telkwa, cross the Bulkley River and then the CN track to join Coalmine Road. After about 6 km, keep left at the fork where Aveling Coalmine Road turns off to the right. Just over 3 km beyond the fork, at the top of a short, steep hill, is the km 0 marker of Goathorn Creek logging road. At the bottom of the hill it passes an inactive coalmine to the right. After crossing Goathorn Creek at **km 2, follow the right fork northerly, up a steep hill and away from the creek. The road gradually circles left, almost back to Goathorn Creek and then south again. Hunter Basin Road is on right, after km 10.**

At the turn-off, the elevation is about 1000 m and from there, the road climbs for 6 km to timberline, at 1500 m, in Hunter Basin, where it forks. To the left, the road crosses Cabinet Creek and climbs steeply for another kilometer to an abandoned mine camp, where it ends at elevation 1750 m. The right fork climbs up the steep, north wall of the basin and onto the ridge. It follows the ridge around the head of Hunter Basin and eventually fades out at the 2000 m level, on the south side, some 3 km from the fork.

COMMENTS:
The logging road to the start of Hunter Basin Road at km 10 is fairly good and not a problem for standard vehicles. An exception could be the steep climb just after the road crosses Goathorn Creek. Washouts and mud slides are always a possibility there.

Hunter Basin Road is an old mining road, extremely rough and muddy in places. Parts of it are actually quite good, but the bad sections make it virtually impassable even with 4-wheel drive. However, a mountain bike can be used to advantage and speeds up the return trip if nothing else. In winter it is a good road to ski up and when snow conditions are favourable, the run down is very enjoyable. Above timberline, the basin is more often than not very wind blown and the skiing may be poor. The road is also well used by snow-mobiles, so it is necessary watch out for them when skiing down.

The high country surrounding Hunter Basin is ideal for hiking. There are lovely views in all directions, particularly towards the Howson Range in the west and the Hudson Bay and Babine Ranges to the northwest and north. To find places to camp within reach of water and wood, it is necessary to

Hiking in Hunter Basin.

drop down into one of the many small valleys that radiate out from the plateau.

Over the ridge to the west of Hunter Basin is a distinctive formation known locally as the Camel Humps, for obvious reasons. Hiking over in that direction is very pleasant. It is also the route to take to pick up Glacis Creek Trail [TR3] that leads to Mooseskin Johnny Lake. Go almost due west so as to pass just south of the Camel Humps, then bear slightly right and head down into the saddle that is the divide between Tenas and Glacis Creeks. The trail is on the true right bank of Glacis Creek at the divide, but it stays up and remains well above the creek that soon drops out of sight into a canyon.

It is also possible to get up out of Hunter Basin via the road to the old mine camp. There is a sketchy trail heading southwesterly up the draw from the camp. It eventually climbs to the crest of a lateral spur that joins the main ridge some distance below the 2300 m main peak south of Hunter Basin. Around the camp and along the spur are the remains of much mining activity, including piles of tailings that still contain interesting mineral samples.

GLACIS CREEK TRAIL [TR3]

LOCATION:
Telkwa Range, near Mooseskin Johnny Lake.

MAPS REQUIRED:
93L/6 Thautil River (1:50,000)
93L/11 Telkwa (1:50,000)
93L Smithers (1:250,000)

ROUTE DESCRIPTION:
This is a connecting trail from Hunter Basin Road [TR2] to Mooseskin
Johnny Lake that provides a direct route between the east and west sections
of the range.

To access the trail, follow Hunter Basin Road to about the 1700 m level
on the ridge at the head of the basin. Leave the road there and continue
climbing gently in a southwesterly direction to the pass that leads into the
basin south of a prominent and unmistakable rock formation, referred to locally as the Camel Humps. Pick the best route to reach the far side of the
basin just south of the Camel Humps. At that point, bear slightly right and
head straight down into the 1450 m saddle that is the divide between Tenas
and Glacis Creeks. The trail at the head of Glacis Creek is only a short distance beyond the creek on the true right bank. It is rather faint at first, but
soon gets better. While the trail does follow the creek downstream, it stays
quite high up on the sidehill and for 4 or 5 km drops only gradually. For the
next couple of kilometers, it heads down more steeply, right to the creek.

Across some of the open, marshy areas higher up and where there are
switchbacks lower down, it is easy to loose the trail occasionally, but most of
the way it is quite well defined.

When it reaches the creek, the trail immediately crosses to the other
side only to re-cross it a short distance downstream. After staying close to the
creek for something less than a kilometer and crossing once more to the
south side, the trail climbs away from the creek, angling up towards the crest
of a ridge that eventually terminates at the north end of Mooseskin Johnny
Lake. There is a small, un-named lake where the trail reaches the crest. After
passing the north end of the lake, the trail at first bears slightly to the right,
but eventually it bears left again, so the net effect is a heading that is generally due west towards the south end of another small lake, some 2 km away. It
has no map name, but is referred to locally as Beaver Lake. The trail between the two little lakes is faint in places, but is well enough blazed and
flagged that it is not too difficult to follow. From Beaver Lake a good trail
runs almost due south for about 2 km to the McIntyre's cabin on Mooseskin
Johnny Lake.

The total distance from the start of Hunter Basin Road to Mooseskin

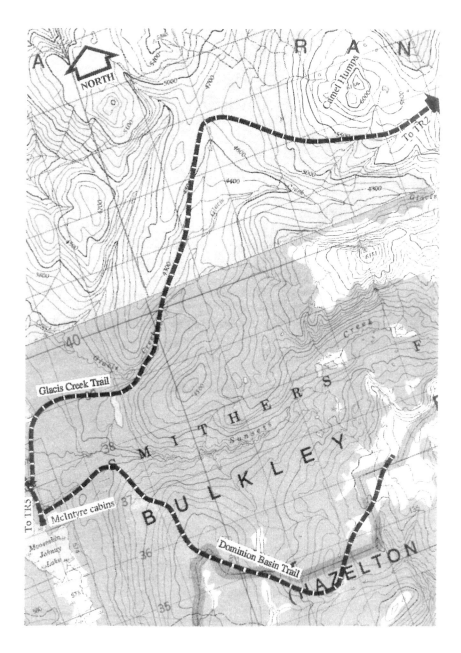

GLACIS CREEK TRAIL [TR3]
DOMINION BASIN TRAIL [TR4]
(Part of Maps 93L/6&11)
1cm=2/3km, 100ft.(30m) contour interval

At the head of Glacis Creek; Camel Humps on the left.

Johnny Lake is in the order of 25 km. In either direction, the trip involves climbing from 1000 m up to almost 1800 m and then dropping down again to 1000 m. It can easily be done in a day, but allow 8-10 hours.

DIRECTIONS:
As for Hunter Basin Road [TR2].

COMMENTS:
This is only one of many trails that was already well developed by 1911 and provided good access to much of the Telkwa Range. The three main routes that led to Mooseskin Johnny Lake were, Glacis Creek Trail coming in from Hunter Basin, another trail up the true left bank of Tenas Creek that joined Glacis Creek Trail and a trail up Telkwa River and Howson Creek [TR5]. There was actually a fourth trail that came up Morice River and Thautil River. From Mooseskin Johnny Lake there were trails to Dominion Basin [TR4], Starr Basin and Howson Basin [TR5], a branch of which went up Evening Creek.

While Glacis Creek Trail is not too bad for hiking, it is no longer a good horse trail and is a poor trail for skiing, particularly going down. Still, it is of considerable interest because it provides access to the country around Mooseskin Johnny Lake and the western section of the Telkwa Range, without the need to cross Telkwa River. On the other hand, if that crossing is feasible, it becomes possible to hike in via Hunter Basin and out along Howson Creek Road or vice versa. Considering that the McIntyres, who live at Mooseskin Johnny Lake year round, have cabins and canoes that they rent out, such a trip can include some fishing and be undertaken without carrying full camping gear.

185

DOMINION BASIN TRAIL [TR4]
(Route map on p.184)

LOCATION:
Telkwa Range, near Mooseskin Johnny Lake.

MAPS REQUIRED:
93L/6 Thautil River (1:50,000)
93L Smithers (1:250,000)

ROUTE DESCRIPTION:
Dominion Basin is at the head of Denys Creek, some 15 km east of Mooseskin Johnny Lake, as the crow flies. However, 9 km from the lake, the trail reaches timberline, at elevation 1500 m, on the ridge between Sunsets and Denys Creeks. Only that part of the trail is described here. What little remains of it higher up on the open ridge, is of no great interest to hikers.

The trail starts off in an easterly direction from the McInyre's cabin. For the first 1.5 km it hardly climbs as it heads across low-lying, swampy ground towards the base of the ridge immediately south of Sunsets Creek. From there it climbs more or less southeasterly up the ridge for a couple of kilometers until at the 1400 m level, it is directly east of the south end of Mooseskin Johnny Lake.

Most of the way up the timber is fairly open and the ground is dry, so the going is good. On top of the ridge, the terrain changes abruptly to an almost flat, dry, mostly open plateau. Just as it reaches the plateau, the trail is on a near easterly heading, but then it makes quite a sharp turn right to head southerly. Because the ground is so hard and dry, the trail is very faint in places. It generally follows an almost imperceptible draw up for perhaps half a kilometer until the ground ahead starts sloping downhill. At that point, the heading changes abruptly to due east. It is joined there by another, very faint trail coming up from the south end of Mooseskin Johnny Lake.

For the next kilometer, the trail continues easterly as it crosses over a low hump and drops down into a marshy depression that is the head of Thautil River. Across the hump, the ground is quite dry and the trail is very good as it winds its way through the semi-open country. Through the marsh, there are a couple of places where it is obscured by the low brush, but with care, it is reasonably easy to follow. After the marsh, the trail heads southeasterly as it starts to work its way around another hump on the ridge. Gradually it bears left again so that on the east side of the hump, it is heading northeasterly. As it circles the hump, the trail goes through some fairly heavy timber, but then it emerges into much more open, semi-alpine terrain. For the last couple of kilometers, until the trail peters out, it climbs gently up the ridge, skirting various small lakes and streams and offers some of the most pleasant hiking to be found anywhere in the Telkwa Range.

Allow 3-4 hours up from Mooseskin Johnny Lake to where the trail fades out and just under 3 hours down.

DIRECTIONS:
For directions on access to Mooseskin Johnny Lake, see Howson Creek Road [TR5] or Glacis Creek Trail [TR3].

COMMENTS:
Dominion Basin trail has been in existence from before 1911 and is part of an extensive trail network that covered the Telkwa Range at that time. Old maps show the trail up from the south end of the lake as the original route, but it is now so badly overgrown and blocked by windfalls that it would need a lot of work to make it passable again.

The ridge accessed by the trail is a wonderful place to hike. It has terrain to suit all, many small lakes, lovely alpine meadows, spectacular views and some great camp sites. It leads directly to a 2340 m peak, surprisingly unnamed, considering it is the highest point in the Telkwa Range.

Relatively recent mineral exploration activies have resulted in a "cat" road being pushed in from the west side of Mooseskin Johnny Lake, across the swamps south of the lake and then southwesterly to Denys Creek. It is still visible, but not much is left of the road, so for access it is virtually useless, but it is shown on the 1:50,000 Thautil River map and could therefore be a helpful landmark, should the need arise.

Sunsets Creek from the far side of Mooseskin Johnny Lake; Dominion Basin Trail goes up the ridge just across the lake.

HOWSON CREEK ROAD [TR5]

(Part of Maps 93L/6&11)

1cm=1km, 100ft.(30m) contour interval

188

HOWSON CREEK ROAD [TR5]

LOCATION:
Telkwa Range, near Telkwa River.

MAPS REQUIRED:
93L/6 Thautil River (1:50,000)
93L/11 Telkwa (1:50,000)
93L Smithers (1:250,000)

DIRECTIONS:
From Telkwa, proceed as for Winfield Creek Road [TR7]. Just short of km 19 is the site where a bridge spanned the Telkwa River to access Howson Creek Road. The bridge was washed out many years ago and the river is not fordable there. However, at km 19, a short road leads down to the river where it can be crossed under favourable conditions, by canoe, on horseback and sometimes even on foot. Needless to say, only those with the right experience and equipment should attempt such a crossing. Bear in mind also that the Telkwa River is liable to rise a metre or more very quickly.

Once across the river, it is not difficult to get through the bush and up to the road. It is 18 km in to the McIntyre's cabin at Mooseskin Johnny Lake. Over that distance, the road only gains 300 m in elevation, to reach 1000 m at the lake, so it is an easy grade all the way. For the most part, the road runs a kilometer or more west of Howson Creek, well up on the hillside. After about 14 km, there is a ford across Howson Creek, just downstream of where it is joined by Scallon Creek. At that point the creek has changed direction to flow from west to east. Less than a kilometer beyond the ford, the road forks. Keep left for Mooseskin Johnny Lake. The north end of the lake comes into view in another couple of kilometers, right after crossing the small creek that flows out of the lake. For the last kilometer or so to the McIntyre's cabin, the route is a trail rather than a road.

The road to the right at the fork climbs quite steeply up a ridge in a southwesterly direction and reaches an old mining camp at elevation 1300 m in about 4 km. From there it is only just over a kilometer along the road to timberline, at 1500 m, on the ridge between Howson and Starr Creeks. The road continues on up the ridge and runs along it for many kilometers. There are numerous branch roads as well that go to various sites where mineral exploration has taken place.

COMMENTS:
The present road, preceded by a an old wagon road and a still older trail, is the main access route to the central region of the Telkwa Range. For that reason it is of considerable interest, in spite of it being somewhat rough and overgrown, and the difficult crossing of Telkwa River.

View from Howson Creek Road.

Howson Range from near end of Howson Creek Road.

Prospecting and mineral exploration have been going on in the area since the end of the last century. By 1911 there was already an extensive network of trails in the Telkwa Range with Mooseskin Johnny Lake as the focal point. Trails went to Hunter Basin (Glacis Creek Trail [TR3]), Dominion Basin [TR4], Starr Basin, Howson Basin and to Morice Lake via Thautil River. At the south end of the lake there was a collection of permanent buildings referred to as Howson City on some old maps! A few remains are still visible.

More recent mineral exploration has resulted in the network of roads, some quite good, others mere "cat" tracks, that cover the ridge west of Mooseskin Johnny Lake. The main road along the ridge provides good access to a large area of interesting hiking country at the heads of Starr, Howson, Scallon and Elliot Creeks, including 2090 m Eagle Peak, that for reasons unknown is one of the few named mountains in the whole Telkwa Range. From the end of the road, near the high point on the ridge, there are spectacular views in all directions, but inevitably, the eye is first drawn to the chain of high peaks to the west. It is the Howson Range, crowned by 2750 m Howson Peak. Flanking it are several other summits, almost as high. In the distance, to the southwest, is Atna Peak, also 2750 m. To the south, beyond Morice Lake, the mountains of the Nanika and Tahtsa area, can be seen. Looking north, Hudson Bay Mountain is the dominant feature. The opportunity to take a good look at the eastern section of the Telkwa Range from the vantage point of the ridge, should not be missed. It will quickly become clear that the area on the far side of Mooseskin Johnny Lake is very attractive for hiking and camping. Dominion Basin Trail in particular, and to a lesser extent Glacis Creek Trail, provide easy access to that area.

The long haul up from Telkwa River and the extensive road network above timberline, makes Howson Creek Road an interesting route for mountain bikes, if the problem of getting them across the river can be overcome. For horse riding and skiing, it is also a good road and if conditions are right, the river crossing should not be a problem.

While the shores of Mooseskin Johnny Lake are generally marshy and discourage camping, there is no shortage of good campsites away from the lake. The best area is along the creek that flows out of it to the north. For those who prefer greater comfort, or wish to avoid carrying full camping gear, the McIntyres, who live year round at the lake, have cabins for rent. They also rent out canoes to those who want to try catching some of the fine rainbow trout that inhabit the lake.

HANKIN PLATEAU TRAIL [TR6]
(Route map on p.178)

LOCATION:
Telkwa Range, near Telkwa.

MAPS REQUIRED:
93L/6 Thautil River (1:50,000)
93L/11 Telkwa (1:50,000)
93L Smithers (1:250,000)

ROUTE DESCRIPTION:
A good trail, starting at elevation 1000 m from km 12 on Goathorn Creek logging road and reaching timberline at 1450 m after 7 km.

For about the first kilometer, the trail is a winter logging road, then it bears right onto an old mining road and follows it for another kilometer or so, all the time parallelling the east fork of Webster Creek. Just after a small creek that has cut a gully across the road, turn sharp left onto a fairly well defined trail through the trees. Within 50 m of the road, bear right onto a much better trail. It is an old mining trail that essentially follows the crest of the ridge, immediately east of the east fork of Webster Creek, all the way to timberline. The trail is quite well defined and easy to find most of the way, but in a couple of places it is necessary to be careful not to lose it. For the first kilometer after leaving the mining road, the trail keeps bearing right as it first climbs quite gently, but eventually starts to drop again. At that point, it is almost heading back towards the road. After crossing a shallow draw, the trail makes a very sharp turn to the left and starts to climb steeply. From the sharp turn, there is an alternate connecting trail heading downhill, in a westerly direction, back to the mining road.

The steep climb goes on, with minor variations in grade and direction, for perhaps a kilometer, then the grade eases and the trail even drops slightly for a short distance before it starts to climb the next step on the ridge. Where the trail drops, there is an unexpected turn to the right before the previous heading is resumed after a very short distance. It is one of the places where it is easy to lose the trail. After a steep climb up the next step, there is a longer, level section, about 2 km from timberline, then the trail bears left as it starts to climb again, not quite so steeply. Here the trail crosses to the east side of the ridge, but as it nears timberline, it heads back towards the west side. Where it leaves the timber, the trail is near the edge of a steep drop-off down towards the east fork of Webster Creek. From the rock outcrop at the edge, there is a great view of the whole creek basin and to the north, out over the Bulkley Valley.

Above timberline the trail fades out, but it is easy going without it, just follow the edge of the plateau up. It should take 2-3 hours to reach open country and perhaps half an hour less to go back down.

DIRECTIONS:

From Telkwa, proceed as for Hunter Basin Road [TR2], but continue on along Goathorn Creek logging road beyond km 10. The road soon starts to drop down and in another 1.5 km crosses Cabinet Creek just downstream of where it is joined by Webster Creek. At the top of the hill on the other side, near km 12, turn right into an open log sorting area. The winter logging road, that is the start of the trail, is the exit closest to the creek. If the ground is not too soft, park in the log sorting area, otherwise use the road.

COMMENTS:

This trail provides good access to an extensive, plateau-like formation. It is a wonderful place to hike and camp. There is no water to be found on the way up along the trail, but above the 1500 m level and away from the ridge that edges the plateau to the west, it is not hard to find campsites with fire-wood, water and a view. Camping on the plateau has the great advantage that there are no mountains in the way of either the morning or the evening sun. At night, the lights of Smithers make a pretty picture as they twinkle and shine far below. The daytime view out over the Bulkley Valley and surrounding mountains is even more impressive.

The plateau rises steadily towards the south where it eventually ends at a steep drop-off into a narrow valley. Far below in the valley-bottom, there is a series of small lakes joined by an un-named creek that is a tributary to Dockrill Creek. The lakes have the deep green colour so characteristic of glacial melt water and are exceptionally photogenic. To the southwest, the plateau narrows to a knife-ridge that seperates the un-named creek from the east fork of Webster Creek. By hiking up the ridge on the west side of the plateau, and after crossing a desolate, rock strewn plain, it is not difficult to access the knife-ridge. At 2000 m, it is also the highest point on the plateau. The ridge is wide enough for walking and provides a reasonable approach route to the 2340 m, un-named summit of the Telkwa Range, only a kilometer or so away to the southwest.

Looking up Webster Creek (East fork) from Hankin Plateau Trail.

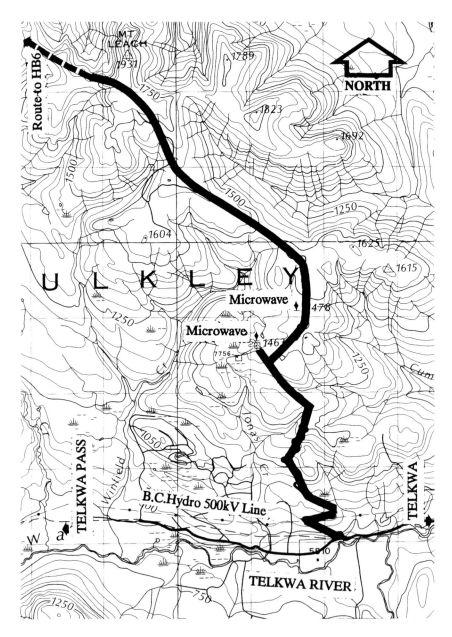

WINFIELD CREEK ROAD [TR7]

(Part of Map 93L/NW)

1cm = 1km , 50m contour interval

WINFIELD CREEK ROAD [TR7]

LOCATION:
Telkwa River, near Telkwa.

MAPS REQUIRED:
93L/11 Telkwa (1:50,000)
93L Smithers (1:250,000)

DIRECTIONS:
Turn southwest off Hwy.16 at Telkwa, cross the Bulkley River, then the CN track and join Coalmine Road. After about 6 km the road forks; take the right fork which is Aveling Coalmine Road. Telkwa River Forest Road starts after another 3 km, but km 0 is back at the fork. At the 8 km sign, the road crosses to the true left bank of Telkwa River and continues upstream, mostly within sight of the river. Just past the 19 km sign, Winfield Creek Road branches off to the right, angling up the steep hillside.

The road is quite well laid out and constructed and normally in a good state of repair. Over a distance of 9 km from the turn-off at elevation 700 m, it climbs on a fairly uniform grade to timberline at 1500 m. Near the bottom, the road goes under the 500 kV power line from Prince George to Terrace. At the top, the road passes B.C.Tel's and B.C.Hydro's microwave stations.

Beyond the high point, the road drops down into a saddle at the head of Winfield Creek and then continues on, climbing gently along the main ridge in a northwesterly direction. It goes on for another 10 km as a "cat" track that in places may be barely negotiable with 4-wheel drive if the ground is wet.

COMMENTS:
Mt.Leach at 1930 m, the highest point on the ridge, is easy to reach from the "cat" track that passes just south of it. There are good views from the top, notably of Howson Range to the southwest and Hudson Bay Range to the north.

In some places the terrain has been badly torn up by wide-ranging surface mineral exploration that will remain an eyesore for decades. However, most of the accessible country is excellent for hiking and camping. It is largely an extensive plateau dissected by small streams and dotted with little lakes. There are some lovely meadows and many interesting rock formations. These features and the easy access makes it a choice area for families with children.

The whole plateau is well suited for ski touring and horse riding. The extensive "cat" track network also makes it an ideal area for mountain biking. Near the end of the "cat" track, the ridge overlooks McDonell Lake. From that point it is possible to link up with the top of McDonell Lake Trail [HB6].

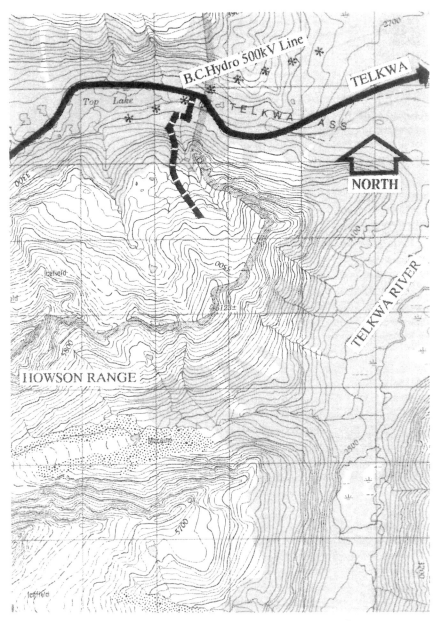

TOP LAKE TRAIL [TR8]

(Part of Map 93L/12)

1cm=1/2km, 100ft.(30m) contour interval

TOP LAKE TRAIL [TR8]

LOCATION:
Telkwa Pass, near Telkwa.

MAPS REQUIRED:
93L/12 Milk Creek (1:50,000)
93L Smithers (1:250,000)

ROUTE DESCRIPTION:
A short, steep trail, starting at elevation 900 m, close to the east end of Top Lake. It reaches timberline at 1200 m, about 2 km south of the lake.

The trail is sketchy in places and not easy to follow. It switchbacks up a very steep slope on the true left bank of an un-named creek. On the map, the creek is shown draining into Top Lake, but in reality it flows the other way and eventually joins the Telkwa River.

Above timberline not much of the trail remains and rather than trying to follow it, simply pick the easiest route up. However, because the slope is so steep and there are some sheer rock faces on either side of the trail below timberline, it is important to leave a few markers so it can be easily located on the way down.

The start of the trail is well concealed by the dense alder that has grown up along the powerline right-of-way where the road also runs. Just after the road first joins the right-of-way, it crosses under the powerline. Looking at the slope due south of the road, from a point near mid-span of the powerline, the trail goes up along the most westerly of the two minor gullies. The simplest way to get there is to charge straight through the alder to the edge of the right-of-way and then continue on for about the same distance through the underbrush to intersect a small creek. It is the same creek that the trail eventually follows. On the other side of it, there are vestiges of a "cat" road that can be followed up along and then back across the creek. After that, it first follows the base of the steep slope in westerly direction away from the creek. Ignore the first side road up the hill to the left, but shortly after that, the road bears left and starts to climb. Less than half a kilometer from the last creek crossing, at the top of a short, steep hill, turn left onto a road heading back towards the creek. The trail starts near the creek at the end of the "cat" road and heads up the hill in a southerly direction.

Allow 2 hours for the hike up to timberline and a good hour down.

DIRECTIONS:
From Telkwa, proceed as for Winfield Creek Road [TR7], but continue on along Telkwa River Forest Road beyond the Winfield Creek Road turn-off. At about km 26, the logging road turns right and heads up Winfield Creek. Take the road straight ahead that fords the creek and continues on to-

Looking through Telkwa Pass from the west.

Mountains north of Telkwa Pass from across Zymoetz River.

wards Telkwa Pass. Beyond the creek for the next 18 km or so, to where the trail starts, the road is fair to poor with some very steep, rough and muddy sections. There are fords across Sinclair, Tsai and Milk Creeks and some other, un-named creeks.

From the Milk Creek ford it is about 5 km to where the road joins the powerline right-of-way and the trail begins.

After a dry spell and late in the season when the creeks are likely to be at their lowest, the road as far as Telkwa Pass may be just passable for 4-wheel drive vehicles. Otherwise it is quite unpredictable how far it is possible to drive. Milk Creek is often a major obstacle, primarily because it is a large, glacier fed tributary to the Telkwa River, but also due to the steep, muddy hill on the east side.

If a mountain bike can be brought along, it certainly speeds progress where the road is no longer drivable.

COMMENTS:

The road through Telkwa Pass was first put in to facilitate construction of a natural gas pipeline and later used for construction of a major powerline. It is not much used by either utility for maintenance access, consequently no work has been done on the road in recent years and it has gradually deteriorated. At one time it was possible to get through all the way from Telkwa to Terrace with a 4-wheel drive vehicle.

A sketchy trail at the end of a long drive on a bad road is not of great interest to most people. It has been included because it is the only reasonably easy ground access to any part of the majestic Howson Range. Unfortunately, the trail only provides access to the northern extremity of the range. Once above timberline, it is not difficult to hike up to an 1800 m saddle in the main ridge, but beyond that it requires technical climbing experience and equipment to continue. In any case it is still a long way from 2750 m Howson Peak. All serious climbing in the Howson Range has been based on float plane access to North Burnie Lake and a forward base camp at Sandpiper Lake.

Telkwa Pass is a narrow, relatively low elevation corridor through high, rugged mountains. It offers some spectacular scenery, but being well below timberline and hemmed in by steep slopes, it has little to offer in the way of hiking.

Anyone considering crossing over the pass on skis, by mountain bike or any other mode of transportation should verify ahead of time that the logging road up along the Zymoetz River from Terrace is passable all the way to Limonite Creek. Not infrequently, sections of that road have been washed out, and completely impassable, just below the Kitnayakwa River junction.

REFERENCES

(1) **Geology of the Northwest Mainland**: Allen Gottesfeld, Kitimat Centennial Museum Association, 1985.

(2) **A Climber's Guide to the Coastal Ranges of British Columbia**: Dick Culbert, The Alpine Club of Canada, 1969 (ed.2).

(3) **Summary Report, p.55**: R.G. McConnell, Geol. Survey of Canada, 1912.

(4) **Summary Report, Pt.A, p.39**: G. Hanson, Geol. Survey of Canada, 1922.

(5) **Summary Report, Pt.A, p.31**: G. Hanson, Geol. Survey of Canada, 1923.

(6) **Kitimat Prior to 1879**: G. Robinson, Cariboo and N.W. Digest, Vol.12, No.6, Nov.-Dec. 1956 & Vol.14, No.3, May-June 1958.

(7) **Tales of Kitamaat**: G. Robinson, ca. 1958.

(8) **Time and Place**: G. Robinson, S. Rough et al., 1958.

(9) **Kitimat My Valley**: Elizabeth Varley, Northern Times Press, 1981.

(10) **The Kitimat Valley**: B.C. Department of Lands, 1913.

(11) **The History of Terrace**: Nadine Asante, Terrace Public Library Association, 1972.

(12) **People of the Snow**: John Kendrick, NC Press, 1987.

(13) The Canadian Alpine Journal, Vol.28, 1941.

(14) **The Tseax Lava Beds**: Kitimat Centennial Museum Association, 1983.

(15) **Skeena River of Destiny**: R. Geddes Large, Gray's Publishing, 1981.

(16) **Mineral Resources of Terrace Area**: E.D. Kindle, Geol. Survey of Canada, Memoir 205, 1936.

(17) **Hiking the Rainforest**: Shannon Mark, Heather McLean, Bookmark Publishers, 1985.

(18) **Mineral Resources, Usk to Cedarvale**: E.D. Kindle, Geol. Survey of Canada, Memoir 212, 1937.

(19) **Mineral Resources, Hazelton and Smithers Areas**: E.D. Kindle, Geol. Survey of Canada, Memoir 223, 1954.

(20) **Geology of the Rocher Deboule Range**: A. Sutherland Brown, B.C. Department of Mines, 1960.

(21) **The History of the Northern Interior of British Columbia, 1660 to 1880**: The Rev. A.G. Morice, Interior Stationery (1970) Ltd., 1978.

(22) **Smithers From Swamp to Village**: R.L.Shervill, Town of Smithers, 1981.

(23) **Bulkley Valley Stories**: Heritage Club, 1973.

(24) **The Telkwa River and Vicinity**: W.W. Leach, Government Printing Bureau, Ottawa, 1907.

(25) The Canadian Alpine Journal, Vol.41, 1958.

(26) The Canadian Alpine Journal, Vol.42, 1959.

(27) **More Trails to Timberline** : Einar Blix, Fjelltur Books, 1994.

(--) **Annual Reports** : B.C. Minister of Mines, 1897 to 1972.

METRIC TO IMPERIAL COVERSION SCALES

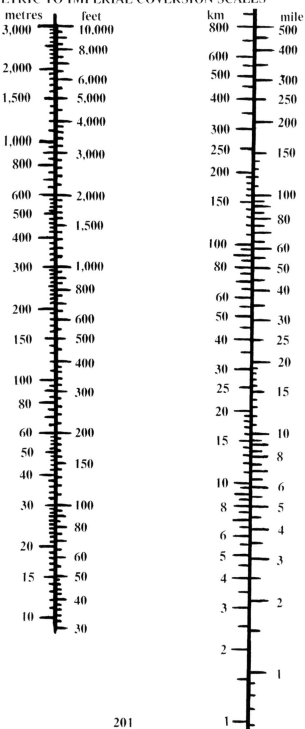

metres	feet
3,000	10,000
	8,000
	6,000
2,000	
1,500	5,000
	4,000
1,000	3,000
800	
600	2,000
500	1,500
400	
300	1,000
	800
200	600
150	500
	400
100	300
80	
60	200
50	150
40	
30	100
	80
20	60
15	50
	40
10	30

km	mile
800	500
600	400
500	300
400	250
300	200
250	150
200	
150	100
	80
100	60
80	50
60	40
50	30
40	25
30	20
25	15
20	
15	10
	8
10	6
8	5
6	4
5	3
4	
3	2
2	1
1	